'*Leading – the Millennial Way* i
examination of what it takes
lennials. The book provides a novel insight into what inspires
and motivates millennials; it challenges the stereotypes that are
frequently used to crudely categorize their attitudes and ambi-
tions. It also describes practical tools to help both pre-millennials
and millennials to become successful leaders. To get the most
from – and for – millennials, read, learn and put into practice
this manual for leading – the millennial way.'

*Dr Ivan Boyd, former Head of Business Engagement
and Operations, Research and Innovation at British Telecom*

'If millennials are to develop into leaders of integrity and influence,
dialogue between the generations about how to help organizations
and people flourish and make an impact will be important. It is
encouraging to see Simon and Rachel model that here for a
balanced perspective on millennials and leadership.'

Tom Christmas, founder and National Coordinator, Just Love

'Simon and Rachel helpfully outline the thoughts and needs of
the millennial generation all over the world. Their approach to
leading and developing millennials is one of grace and humility
that will bring the best out of this talented, but often misunderstood, group of people.'

Ben Cooley, CEO, Hope for Justice

'There's nothing new "under the sun" and so, of course, every
generation wants to "crack the code" and get the most out of
life. This helpful, thoughtful book suggests that because millennials
are asking questions, and even suggesting answers, previous

generations have skated over, they are well placed to provide a better breed and brand of leadership. I hope that is true!'

Each year, tens of thousands of millennial volunteers and employees serve in Christian camps around the world. This book is transformational in helping us to understand how millennials think and act, how they are motivated and how they learn, how they lead and how they like to be led. It will be used globally to inform and educate those working with millennials.

'*Leading – the Millennial Way* is a powerful read, written in a real, raw and engaging style. Its insightful and practical approach offers clarity in a changing landscape and creates positive bridges of understanding between generations. This is essential reading for existing and aspiring leaders in any context.'

'This book leaves me with one overwhelming thought: I want more millennials in my organization, so I need to encourage millennials to lead. I commend this book to all leaders and potential leaders, whether from the millennial generation or not. Reflective and research-based, practical and perceptive, this is a book to transform your thinking and actions.'

'This is important research and a significant book. Coming from the context of public sector leadership, I was struck not by the evolution of this new generation of leaders (their expectations, enhanced capabilities and dynamic energy) but by the organizational incongruence of many of the workplaces they are now entering. So, we must engage with this data and listen carefully to their narrative and the thought-provoking dialogue between Barrington and Luetchford. Within this book lies a challenge for personal renewal and, more significantly, for workplace reinvention and revolution. It is clear that we are in rough waters. This a book to help us to ride those difficult waves.'

Dr Rob Loe, CEO, Relationships Foundation

'*Leading – the Millennial Way* provides us with highly valuable insights into the millennial mindset. This book should be on the reading list of leaders – of every generation – interested in identifying the skills required to lead well in our rapidly changing and challenging world.'

David McCahon, senior lawyer at a FTSE 100 company

'This is a timely book that every team should read. If we hope to collaborate successfully and construct a culture of respect and understanding across generations, *Leading – the Millennial Way* is the perfect building tool. Packed with information and inspiration, it made me exclaim "Yes – that's so true!" on many occasions. I will be referring to this book again and again and using it in many contexts – I wholeheartedly recommend that you do the same.'

Cathy Madavan, author, speaker, coach and member of Kyria Network Council of Reference

'In *Leading – the Millennial Way*, Simon and Rachel use years of experience combined with up-to-date research to give us a unique book that contains expert analysis. If you are serious about seeing culture transformed, you need to read this book. It is insightful, practical and inspiring. I thoroughly recommend it.'

Patrick Regan OBE, founder and CEO, Kintsugi Hope

'A thoughtful and timely book that gets to the heart of a crisis in leadership and navigates a way forward. I recommend it for anyone looking for solutions with practical, deep and insightful truths for every generation.'

Danielle Strickland, speaker, author and social justice advocate

'As Simon and Rachel's insights about the millennial organization and millennial leader unfolded, I found myself exclaiming out loud. Their book makes sense of what I, as a non-millennial, experience when leading millennials and interacting with millennial leaders. A "must-read" for those seeking to live out their purpose at work with authenticity and integrity, and who want to help those they work with to create an environment in which leadership is service, and integrity is everything.'

Joëlle Warren MBE, Executive Chair, Warren Partners

'Baby boomers and Generation X are well researched and (allegedly) well understood. But what about those of the subsequent generation? We call them millennials, but do we really understand them? More importantly, do we know how to lead them? Using quantitative research, Simon and Rachel start by exploring what a millennial isn't and debunk a number of myths. A thoroughly practical book that includes an array of tips, *Leading – the Millennial Way* really helps the leader of today and the future. Entertaining and informative.'

Andrew Williams, Partner, Maisha + Co

LEADING –
THE MILLENNIAL WAY

Simon Barrington
with
Rachel Luetchford

To Andrew + Lesley

Every Blessing

First published in Great Britain in 2019

Society for Promoting Christian Knowledge
36 Causton Street
London SW1P 4ST
www.spck.org.uk

British Library Cataloguing-in-Publication Data
A catalogue record for this book is available from the British Library

ISBN 978–0–281–08077–9
eBook ISBN 978–0–281–08076–2

Typeset by Manila Typesetting Company
First printed in Great Britain by Jellyfish Print Solutions
Subsequently digitally printed in Great Britain

eBook by Manila Typesetting Company

Produced on paper from sustainable forests

Contents

About the authors

Simon Barrington studied Physics and Music at Cardiff University before becoming Programme Director at British Telecom and, subsequently, for the UK Government Cabinet Office. He became Executive Director (CEO) of Samaritan's Purse – an international relief and development organization – in 2003, a post he held for more than 13 years. During this time, Simon studied for a Master's degree in Global Leadership at Fuller, California. After leaving Samaritan's Purse in May 2017, he founded Forge Leadership Consultancy Ltd, which he currently leads. Simon lives with his wife Heather in Suffolk and they have two grown-up children.

Rachel Luetchford is a millennial who has been interested in issues of social justice from a young age. Before going to university, she went on the Soul Edge leadership course in Canada. She graduated in 2017 with a first-class degree in International Development and is committed to working to provide restorative aftercare for survivors of human trafficking. Rachel is passionate about enabling her generation to make the greatest contribution possible to tackling injustice and transforming society by raising up leaders. While she was the key researcher on the Forge Leadership research report, she interviewed 50 millennials in leadership. She lives with her husband in Suffolk.

Definitions

Millennial
Millennial is a term given to a specific generation of people who reached young adulthood in the first two decades of the millennium. There is a variation over the specific dates. However, for the purposes of this book, millennials will be identified as people born between 1984 and 2000. This fits in with the majority of millennial classifications.

Leadership
Leadership does not necessitate you to have a specific title or position. It is rather how you as a person significantly affect the thoughts, actions and beliefs of the individuals around you. Leaders engage and develop others while working towards a common goal.

Millennial leader
A millennial leader is a millennial (a person born between 1984 and 2000) who is in a position of influence. They may be leading anyone of any age.

Leaders of millennials
Leaders of millennials are non-millennials who are in a position of influence in leading millennials, among others.

Leading the millennial way
Leading the millennial way is a particular style of leadership that will be most effective when used with millennials and may be utilized by millennial leaders or leaders of millennials.

Prologue

Simon: Right now, millennial leaders are in the process of stepping into some of the most significant global leadership roles in businesses, the public sector and charities. Many are already there.

Millennial leaders have shared with us over the past year some of the extreme conditions that they are leading in.

They describe a strong wind blowing whose energy seems diverse, different and difficult to harness. A wind that has been labelled and categorized as people who don't understand it have tried to contain it. It is changing the landscape and blowing where it wills.

This wind is the millennial generation – full of energy, dynamic, hard to put in a box, strong, wild and, critically, whose huge potential has yet to be fully tapped.

All of this in a global economic, social and political environment of rapid change, in a business world where the tectonic plates have moved and created a massive tsunami of volatility, uncertainty, chaos and ambiguity.

The questions both Rachel (a millennial leader) and I (a non-millennial) ask and answer in this book are:

As a millennial leader, how should you lead in a way that best harnesses the incredible potential of your generation?

As a leader of millennials, how can you best harness this potential in those you lead?

And finally:

As an older leader, how do you learn to lead the 'millennial way' and harness the power of a generation?

The key to this, we believe, is dialogue and understanding, which is why we wrote this book.

Where millennial leaders and older leaders have collided and conflicted in trying to navigate the shifts in leadership, this book and the research at its heart is intended to help all leaders better understand and champion leading – the millennial way.

If the millennial generation signals a new force of wind, we believe all leaders can be windsurfers. Empowering you with the strength, skill and dexterity to adapt to changing conditions, the tools in this book will enable you to harness this dynamic energy.

Moving forward with huge momentum, full of integrity, a clear identity, insight and creativity, millennial leaders inspire with daring achievements.

Do you want to harness the power of this incredible generation to ride the waves?

Introduction

Rachel: As a millennial, I've grown up believing that community, family and living purposefully are of the utmost importance. I see myself as a whole person. The person who sits in my favourite coffee shop with my friends is the same person who shows up at work and church and family gatherings.

Although no two millennials are the same (something that the media and many others have often failed to portray), the research I have been conducting with Forge Leadership over the past year, shared throughout this book, does help to paint a picture of the shared-leadership style of our generation. By understanding our core beliefs, we can see the massive potential contribution that our generation can make towards transforming leadership and society.

Simon: Unlike Rachel, my own, and many of my generation's, experience has been centred on careers in performance-oriented, profit-focused organizations. At 22, I poured myself into my first corporate job at the expense of family, friends, children and life: working flat out, desperate to finally reach Friday night, longing to be our real selves for 24 hours before the next Monday morning came hurtling towards us to whisk us away to our alternative reality, where we were forced to wear 'professional' masks.

This contrast is just one of many between old styles of leadership and millennial leadership that can result in conflict in the workplace as we seek to navigate these changes. At Forge Leadership, however, we believe that increased understanding and dialogue between the generations will enable us all to thrive in this new environment. This is why we decided to conduct in-depth original research into the ways and wants of millennial leaders.

The research took place in late 2017 and throughout 2018 in collaboration with Bible Society and Redcliffe College. We interviewed 50 millennials face to face who are already in leadership and surveyed a further 442 millennial leaders online. (You can read more about our method at the back of this book and access all the research at <www.millennial-leader.com/research>.)

We hope our findings will empower millennial leaders to better understand their unique marks, to strengthen their leadership approach and thrive in our ever-changing organizations.

We also think the findings discussed in this book will be of great benefit to those non-millennials who lead millennials or want to learn how to lead the millennial way. Though a new leadership landscape can be unsettling for some who are used to what they know, as we have researched the way in which millennials are now leading, I find myself at home in this world, excited at the types of leadership styles emerging.

During my time as a leader, my leadership style and the whole emphasis of my leadership has gone through a significant revolution, and I am being transformed from the inside out as a result. Though change always takes some getting used to, I now seek to embody and champion 'leading the millennial way'. If you, like me, are a Gen Xer (born between 1961 and 1983) or a baby boomer leader (born between 1945 and 1960), then I hope that my experience will encourage and inspire you to make that transition too. I find many of my peers joining me on the journey, but also many being unnecessarily left behind.

In exploring leading – the millennial way, Part one of the book looks at the environment of work as we now find it, the large strategic changes that are affecting the workplace, and eight significant and seismic shifts that are shaping the very landscape in which millennials are leading.

Part two then draws heavily on the millennial leadership research to expose existing myths about millennials, identify first their core beliefs and then the four key characteristics or marks of millennial leaders that will enable them to succeed in this radically different eco-system.

Finally, Part three sets out practical tools and approaches that can enable leaders to lead 'the millennial way' so that they can transform both culture and their influence. We then set a challenge for millennials and those who are leading them to step up and make the significant difference that they've been prepared for and are ready to make.

Part one

THE ENVIRONMENT MILLENNIALS ARE LEADING IN

Chapter one

THE GROUND IS SHIFTING

Simon: Aged 21, I woke up in the middle of the night in the midst of a 6.8 magnitude earthquake on the fifth floor of a high-rise building in Taiwan. The tectonic plates had collided and my known world was thrown into immediate chaos as all around me buildings shook. In a similar way, trembling exists in our workplaces. The leadership environments of old and new collide, tension and conflict arising as we all learn to navigate this new terrain. This tension was exemplified when we interviewed millennial leader Jon Gosden.

Jon is 29 years old and has already been in business for over a decade. Beginning his business career while still at school with a web-hosting enterprise run from his bedroom, he scaled it up to more than a hundred clients before he left university. Following this, Jon became a Technology Consultant and then Senior Consultant in a very short period of time. He is currently working for a technology company that specializes in transforming the way organizations utilize technology to use their data.

Jon described to us the environment he works in:

> I work for a big tech company that is very flat organizationally, so it means that the best idea always wins and people are fairly collaborative. I don't respond well to being told what to do and most people I work with don't either, so it has to be a shared growing vision of how we could do something better. The approaches that work here are being open and transparent with what we are thinking, getting everyone's views and working together. I spend most of my time, though, working

with governments, which tend to be the opposite. They can be very hierarchical, so bringing people with you is much harder. It's a difficult balance between two very different cultures and trying to bridge that is hard. I'm trying to be more relational and therefore have more influence.

I think that millennials by nature care a lot less about structure and traditional hierarchies and look for much more informal and relational ways of doing things. We also care a little less about traditional roles, titles and status, which means that it's easier for millennials to lead in the position they are in rather than feeling they have to be anointed to lead. I think that's often where some of the most innovative work happens.

Over the past generation, we have witnessed dramatic changes in social structures, politics, world views and culture that continue to develop rapidly today. And as Jon's interview further highlights, the world of work is no exception to these changes.

Frederic Laloux, in his insightful and challenging work, *Reinventing Organizations*, identifies this shift in organizational structure and culture as a move towards a new level of organizational consciousness. This new way of working recognizes the change in the order of 'seeking' in our lives.

Recognition, success, wealth and belonging are no longer the primary things that are sought after. Rather, 'we pursue a life well-lived, and the consequences might just be recognition, success, wealth and love'.[1]

Laloux goes on to describe three breakthroughs in organizational structure that he identified in his research, and which categorize the type of organizations that millennials are seeking to lead.

1 Self-management
Learning to operate effectively, even at a large scale, with a system based on peer relationships and without the need for either hierarchy or consensus.

2 Wholeness
Developing a consistent set of practices that invite us to reclaim our inner wholeness and bring all of who we are to work, rather than leaving parts of ourselves at home.

3 Evolutionary purpose
Members of the organization are invited to listen to and understand what the organization, which is regarded as a living organism, wants to become, what purpose it wants to serve and to adapt the organization accordingly.

Rachel: This emerging organizational revolution feels almost intuitive for many of us among the millennial generation. In a survey of nearly 7,700 millennials globally in 2016, Deloitte found 87 per cent of us were saying that 'the success of a business should be measured in terms of more than just its financial performance'[2] and yet 54 per cent believed businesses around the world 'have no ambition beyond making money'. The issue of purpose in organizational life has become a critical one.

We want to contribute to the positive impact business has on society, but in so doing, we wish to stay true to our personal values. Therefore, we tend to choose organizations whose values reflect our own – a concept reinforced by Deloitte in finding that, globally, 56 per cent of millennials have 'ruled out ever working for a particular organization because of its values or standard of conduct', which don't align with their own.

Simon: Aaron Sachs and Anupam Kundu of Thoughtworks[3] have identified five key mind-shifts in the landscape and environment in which millennials are being asked to lead. Whereas Sachs and Kundu identify these as shifts, they are in reality polarities that organizations are seeking to navigate and hold in tension. It is not so much a move from profit *to* purpose (for example) but the need to hold in tension profit *and* purpose.

Our world is full of such polarities. You may call them paradoxes, dilemmas or tensions. These are seemingly opposing views or poles, which it is tempting to think that we have to make black and white decisions between. Competent leaders both within and of the millennial generation are increasingly learning to manage these polarities effectively. Such leaders are mastering how to both centralize for coordination and decentralize for responsiveness. They are also learning the difference between solving a problem and managing a tension, a big mistake to get the wrong way round, yet many seeking to regain control in this uncertain environment can too often confuse them. Leading the millennial way is arguably more about learning to manage polarities well rather than quick and definitive problem-solving.

Sachs and Kundu's five polarities
Here are the five polarities that Sachs and Kundu identify as shifts.

1 Profit and purpose
Organizations are becoming more holistic in their outlook and embracing the need for a balanced view of the sustainable good they are having on society.

2 Hierarchies and wirearchies
Organizations are becoming more networked and collaborative in the search to become more agile and responsive to huge change.

3 Planning and creativity
Organizations are becoming more creative and embracing wider circles of diversity of thinking to create improved outcomes.

4 Gut instinct and experimentation
Organizations are becoming more experimental in their approach, using digital technologies to experiment, fail quickly, learn and adapt.

5 Privacy and transparency
Organizations are becoming more transparent: to their customers, to their employees and to their shareholders.

The Forge Leadership's additional three polarities
In addition to these polarities, our original research has identified a further three polarities in the workplace environment, which are given here.

1 Flexibility and community
Organizations are becoming more aware of the need to balance the drive for flexible working with the motivational and productivity benefits of building community.

2 Whole-hearted commitment and whole-life flourishing
Organizations are becoming more committed to the whole-life well-being of their employees and are seeking to balance this with the need for whole-hearted commitment in the workplace.

3 Safety and challenge
Organizations are realizing the need to create 'safe' spaces in which people feel trusted and that this builds greater levels of productivity and creativity, at the same time as creating environments that are high in challenge.

There are many great organizations that are holding these polarities in bold tension as they seek to navigate the shifting environment they are working in. There are others that are particularly good at one but struggle to navigate the rest.

'Shaking' organizations

In Parts two and three, we will look at *why* our organizations are 'shaking' as a result of the collision and contrast between old and new styles of leadership. But, before we do, it's important to survey the landscape to better understand the dynamic developments at play.

As you read on, ask yourself the questions:

- Where are the foundations of my organization being shaken right now?
- Which of these tensions is causing the most angst in my organization at the moment?

Chapter two

MARKS OF THE MILLENNIAL ORGANIZATION - KNOWING YOUR LEADERSHIP LANDSCAPE

FLEXIBILITY AND COMMUNITY

Rachel: Peek through the window at my local coffee shop and you will spot many individuals with their laptops plugged in and their headphones on. A latte, flat white or mocha takes them through the morning while they conduct business around the world over Zoom or Skype, participate in conference calls, finish reports and presentations, send emails and fuel the 'gig' economy.

In those coffee shops there is a sense, even to a small degree, of being part of a community of fellow workers.

Millennial leaders told us that they are inherently relational, with 94 per cent saying that the quality of relationships in the workplace is important or extremely important to them (see Figure 2.1 overleaf).

Simon: This strong desire for relationship is a counterpoint to the drive to allow workers more flexibility in their working patterns.

Over the past decade, the pace of life, the demand for greater work–life balance and the increasing availability of good wireless connectivity has meant that the ability to roam and work has become a norm for a growing number of mainly professional employees.

How important to you is the quality of your relationships in the workplace?
442 respondents

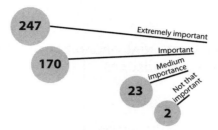

Figure 2.1 Importance of quality of relationships in the workplace

Flexible working has also given employees a sense of more control over their work day and work environment, and has therefore reduced their stress levels and allowed them to work when they accomplish most, feel at their freshest and enjoy working.

And there have been significant benefits to businesses as well, with decreased office space requirements, the ability to hire people from a wide variety of locations, increased staff retention and morale and a heightened reputation as an employer of choice.

It's not all a bed of roses though.

The lack of clear delineation between work and home and the blurring of boundaries is a significant issue for employees to navigate. Expectations can also be harder to manage and there can be feelings of guilt for being in the supermarket at 11 a.m., even though you were up and starting work at 6.30 a.m. while everyone else was just leaving home for the commute to the workplace. There is also a FOMO on relationships and friendships in the office.

Rachel: In our online survey, less than 25 per cent of leaders said they were beyond satisfied with their work–life balance and more than a third of us said we were less than satisfied. Even with the widespread introduction of flexible working, which I love, there is still a significant issue (see Figure 2.2).

How satisfied are you with your own work–life balance at the moment?
442 respondents

Figure 2.2 Satisfaction with work–life balance

When those who were only partly or not at all satisfied with their work–life balance were asked the reason for their dissatisfaction, 39 per cent answered that it was because the boundaries between work and life are very blurred (see Figure 2.3 overleaf).

I have struggled with these blurred boundaries. In fact, I had to stop myself reading all my work emails on the morning of my wedding because they come to my personal phone and I habitually check them!

This came up in several interviews with fellow millennials too. One, we'll call him Tim, founded and directs a UK charity working on social justice issues he is passionate about. There is a sense, according to Tim, in which if this matters so much then why shouldn't one give all one's time to it? Tim says:

A lot of my friends are also involved in the work that I do. It's a common conversation topic even in social settings . . . so my brain is always on it, and it can be hard to switch off.

If you are only partly or not at all satisfied with your work–life balance, what is the main problem creating your dissatisfaction?
253 respondents

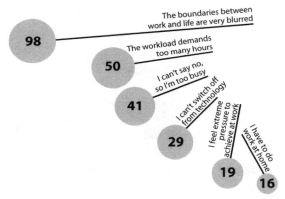

Figure 2.3 Reasons for dissatisfaction with work–life balance

Simon: It's clear that relationships are most important in millennial leaders' minds and, if organizations are to make adjustments that are more than a white-washing of the walls, they must focus on more radical changes that enable deep levels of community and ensure their organizations are relational to the core.

Pixar must be one of the most creative companies on the planet and I've spent many an hour laughing and enjoying the incredible visual feasts they serve up. Ed Catmull, the president of Pixar, in 'How Pixar Fosters Collective Creativity', an article in the *Harvard Business Review*, attributed the studio's success in creating a string of highly popular animated films to its 'vibrant community where talented people are loyal to one another and their collective work, everyone feels that they are part of something extraordinary, and their passion and accomplishments make the community a magnet for talented people coming out of schools or working at other places.'[1]

Similarly, Google encourages its employees to become teachers and coach one another to help build a more creative, satisfied and intimate community.

Facebook is going a step further by building housing, a retail park and amenities at its new headquarters in Menlo Park, California. The intention is to build a community where employees can play, work and rest, have little distance to travel to work and can interact with one another in social as well as work settings.

Millennial leaders are flocking to work for these companies as a result.

The challenge for organizations today who want to encourage millennials to engage and who want to lead in a 'millennial way' is to hold in tension the increased demand for flexible working with all its benefits and challenges, with the need to create vital, vibrant communities of employees that support one another through increased levels of authentic relationships.

PROFIT AND PURPOSE

Rachel: In our online survey, 86 per cent of millennial leaders thought it was extremely or very important that the purpose of the organization matched their own sense of purpose.

My mum humorously tells the story of trying to navigate a conversation with me about Global South debt when I was three years old! I was upset by seeing homeless people in our town, which led to talking about global injustice.

When I was 17, I climbed Kilimanjaro and visited Kibera Slum in Nairobi to raise money for a development charity's efforts there. I have since volunteered with charities that seek to reduce and eradicate poverty, have interned for an anti-human-trafficking charity, worked in Greece in refugee camps and alongside a native people group in Canada struggling with gang crime and addiction.

This sense of purpose in caring for the vulnerable and seeking justice runs through me and is something I utilize and don't ignore when making life decisions. Purpose is a key word for many millennials. *Why* are we doing what we are being asked to do?

Simon: In research undertaken by Cranfield School of Management and The Doughty Centre in 2014, they interviewed current and future business leaders, asking them what the key indicators of business success are now and in the future. The research concluded: 'Both generations perceive profitability and shareholder value as indicators of current business success. However, while current leaders believe these will remain key, future leaders believe future indicators of success will include societal and environmental impact, innovation and development of talent, all of which reflect integration of social purpose into the business.'[2] Business leaders are beginning to answer the question: what game are we trying to win?

Is it good enough to just beat this quarter's financial performance expectations, or is there a greater purpose that truly great companies can aspire to?

For me, I found my greater purpose in work, the 'why' behind what I was doing, in 2000. It was in the middle of 14 years of leadership in the telecommunications industry when I took a trip to the Philippines with the Christian relief and development organization Tearfund.

We spent the afternoon visiting Smokey Mountain, a rubbish tip near Manila harbour that was home to over 4,000 families; families who made their living scavenging among the garbage that had been collected from Metro Manila, a sprawling city of two million inhabitants. The children had scabs and sores and scars, their hair was tinged yellow and their stomachs bloated from malnutrition. Tearfund were running medical clinics and providing much needed inoculations and medicine at the makeshift venue.

As we left the squalor, we walked down to Manila harbour, where a nine-year-old girl approached us. She was dressed in rags and barefoot, the torn T-shirt that she did wear barely covering her dirty and grubby torso, her eyes saddened by the weight of misery she bore at far too young an age. Through an interpreter, she asked me what I did.

How could I possibly explain to this girl that I drove shareholder value for a multinational telecommunications company that made telephones and computing equipment?

Something broke that day; something that asked the deep, fundamental question: what am I doing with my life? My reality had come face to face with a larger purpose that would ultimately take me out of telecommunications and into a role as the chief executive of a large international relief and development organization that would make a turnaround happen for these children.

I chose to fulfil a purpose that was more aligned with my values. Others, whom I applaud, have chosen to stay in corporates and see their corporate purposes transformed and the enormous value they can bring to tackling some of the largest issues on the planet.

Rachel: The massive challenge for millennials is to make the whole of society part of this transformation towards purpose, so that people in my generation don't have to leave and join a charity, because businesses will all be driven towards long-term sustainability.

The rise of corporate social responsibility has been a step in that direction and many large businesses have made strides towards enabling employees to participate in charitable events, to volunteer for charities and to challenge the business contribution to wider society, through sustainable environmental policies and providing life-long care for their employees and communities.

However, you only have to look at the profiteering from large, senior executive salaries and the gender pay gap to see that there is a long, long way to go. We are wanting change and often change that is faster and bolder than previous generations have envisaged or allowed. What might that look like in practice?

Simon: There are always pioneers and my friend, Mark Thomas has been one of them in terms of balancing profit and purpose. In my experience, his example is a rare 'outlier' from my generation, but one that millennial leaders are now seeking to mainstream.

Mark has run a successful small business, MDNFusion, for 25 years. It has been profitable and has also invested in improving the lives of vulnerable children and orphans in Bangladesh and India. Mark explained to me on the Forge Leadership podcast how he balances the need for profit and purpose.[3]

For me, profit is not the primary purpose of business. I fundamentally believe in making profit, but I also believe in using those profits to benefit the people who work in the business and to provide development to other people within society.

MDNFusion provides an excellent leadership assessment service and sets out to make a profit. It also sets out to provide the best possible service and, when we don't provide the best possible service to people, we don't charge.

We have a formula whereby we take a percentage of the revenue of the business – currently eight per cent – which then goes into a charitable fund. The fund is administered by the people in the business and is used to help develop individuals and also goes towards international development.

The aim is to get up to ten per cent of revenue. Therefore we have to be more successful, more profitable than most organizations to survive.

For me, the key thing in leadership is to know what your passions are and your purpose in life for which the skills you are good at are given.

Similarly, in our research, one millennial leader explained, 'We don't respond well to being told to do a task if we aren't captured by the reasons as to why that matters.'

HIERARCHIES AND WIREARCHIES

Rachel: Collaboration came out strongly in the Forge Leadership research, with 90 per cent of millennial leaders saying that it was important or extremely important. It's our natural inclination (see Figure 2.4 overleaf).

In other research, millennial leaders have also shown a tendency for teamwork, collaboration and less hierarchical structure,[4] and

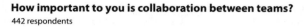

How important to you is collaboration between teams?
442 respondents

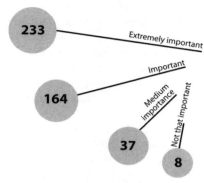

Figure 2.4 The importance of collaboration

we are seen as having an 'above average ability' to work in teams too.[5]

Chou[6] further argues that we adopt participative leadership within the workplace and suggests that millennials desire people-centric leaders who work collaboratively with less regard to boundaries, as opposed to previous, more hierarchical styles.[7] [8]

The appeal of collaboration is strong for millennials, partly because we can see the bigger global picture and can visualize the collaborative impact we could have and how technology and connectedness can make it happen. We therefore won't be satisfied with silo-based thinking.

Simon: The impact of a globally connected, wired world goes way beyond our ability to access information from anywhere and everywhere at the click of a button. We have seen the rise, fall and rise of social media, blogging, vlogging, online shopping and banking, and the rise of a vast networked range of information-gathering and dissemination.

Bill Gates envisioned this in his prophetic work, *Business @ the Speed of Thought* back in 1999 and much of his foresight has come true, with information available to executives in real time to enable decisions on marketing campaigns, capital investments and product placement in ways that previous generations could only have dreamed (or had nightmares) about.[9]

This has led to the ability for people to organize and connect across continents, time-zones and industries and bring the full force of creativity, knowledge, information and application to the most demanding of problems.

The rise of the 'gig' economy is one example of how businesses can now hire anyone at anytime from anywhere to undertake tasks such as web design, translation, transcribing, logo creation and rebranding of whole organizations through apps such as Fivver.

This ability of anyone from anywhere to start a movement that has no headquarters, but rather is a matrix of inter-connected processors and actors, has led to the rise of crypto-currencies, the capacity to enable the Arab Spring and the generation of a global information leak through Wikileaks.

In daily life, it has enabled influencers to influence from any-where, to start petitions and campaigns, to make ideas go viral, and it's allowed people to connect with those who share the same values and purpose regardless of their geography, timezone or socio-economic position.

Rachel: My brother, a fellow millennial, is an example of this. Utilizing what he had, a camera and laptop, he started making YouTube videos, constantly gaining more followers to the point where he has signed with a management company as a social media influencer. No headquarters, no staff introducing him to the right contacts, but the use of the globally connected world and constant engagement on social media with his followers. He is now sent free clothes and products to advertise from companies spotting the power of these interconnected digital spaces, and has just been on his first tour as a presenter.

In their ground-breaking book, *The Starfish and the Spider*, Ori Brafman and Rod A. Beckstrom argue that organizations fall into two categories: traditional 'spiders', which have a rigid hierarchy and top-down leadership, and revolutionary 'starfish', which rely on the power of peer relationships. If you cut off a spider's leg, it's crippled; if you cut off its head, it dies. But if you cut off a starfish's leg it grows a new one, and the old leg can grow into an entirely new starfish.[10]

This is one factor in a complex web impacting the erosion of the effectiveness of command and control as the dominant model for leading and managing purposeful organized activities. The erosion of trust in power, the desire to find meaning and purpose, the ability to lead from anywhere in an eco-system and the constantly shifting landscape of work are also contributors.

In this new environment, millennial leaders are increasingly challenged by the need to manage relationships both within and outside the organization in an authentic way, creating the environment in which a matrix of interconnecting relationships can channel creativity and innovation from anyone to anywhere, without the need for hierarchical organization charts and authoritative command structures.

Various organizational design principles have emerged to help millennial leaders face up to these challenges. 'Wirearchy' is one of them, which the organizers define as:

A dynamic two-way flow of power and authority based on knowledge, trust, credibility and a focus on results, enabled by interconnected people and technology.[11]

Wirearchy is an emergent organizing principle that informs the ways that purposeful human activities and the structures in which they are contained is evolving from top-down direction and supervision (hierarchy's *command-and-control*) to *champion-and-channel* . . . championing ideas and innovation, and channelling time, energy, authority and resources to testing those ideas and the possibilities for innovation carried in those ideas.[12]

This has huge challenges for leaders, as they seek to benefit from the possibilities of open networks of people and process and move towards a culture that is better characterized by increased levels of teamwork, collaboration and operating in ongoing and constant feedback loops.

Flexibility, agility, co-creation, curation, participation and responsiveness become key watchwords for millennial leaders, and the 'soft skills' of relationship management, cultivation and development become critical and require deepening levels of dialogue and listening. Together, we can surely all achieve more, have much more impact and reach our purpose. So why not collaborate? Why not work together to reach some of these goals that otherwise seem annoyingly out of reach?

PLANNING AND CREATIVITY

Rachel: I remember the excitement around the office among my fellow millennials when the leadership team invited anyone to submit a proposal for a new project within our Greek refugee response work. The best idea would be chosen and put into motion, so staff were encouraged to create and innovate, then see those projects come to life. We were excited at being part of the vision and planning of something and it created a sense of ownership, collaboration and ultimately better outcomes.

Similarly, in my interviews with millennials, one millennial expressed to me his amazement at the creative space he was given within his work saying, 'I've just been blown away by the releasing of the director.' He expressed his delight and surprise at being given access to decisions and planning for a large event in his organization's calendar. He said: 'I expected the guys to do it who had experience, but it's very much, "No, we trust you, we want you to do this, we're going to just throw you in there", and I think, for me, that just really demonstrates value.'

For us, planning is a relational activity. We love vision, we love purpose, but we want to be involved in the creation, adaptation and adoption of those plans. Transparency and engagement are key.

Simon: In an increasingly interconnected and rapidly flowing world, linear cause-and-effect planning is showing its age. Involving people in scenario planning that creates stories and options for alternative futures, then bringing them together through active participation in creating those futures, is becoming a vital tool in ensuring that plans are not out of date the moment they are written but are live documents and live explorations of future desired states.

Many businesses have long ago dropped the concept of developing five-year plans or, if they do create them, they are now reviewed at least six monthly and reimagined at least yearly. The pace of change now inherent in business demands alternative approaches.

My American colleagues, especially those involved in disaster relief, never favoured long-term plans and well-worked-out strategies.

The joke used to go that in a disaster, the Americans would arrive within 12 hours and make up the plan as they hit the ground, adapting and refining it as they went, building on experience, local knowledge, gut instinct and creativity, and the Brits would arrive three months later with a well-thought-through plan that would never work in practice.

One fantastic thing I learned though from Ken Isaacs, Vice President of global programmes at Samaritans's Purse, was the value of setting 'river banks' for the operation, especially in a fast-moving, dynamic and changing environment. Although your teams may not know moment by moment what they are going to do next, they always have the 'river banks' in place to ensure that the decisions they are making are in line with the general direction of travel of the organization.

In fast-moving organizations, 'river banks' of operation are initiated through which rivers of creativity can flow within the broad and evolving edges of a defined purpose and direction. Within the 'river banks' are often operating principles, values, sectors of work, species of products, markets or geographies in which the organization will operate. Within that there is flexibility for millennial leaders to experiment and bring creative approaches to determine the organization's evolutionary purpose.

Millennial leaders seek increased connectivity, increased and continual feedback, increased participation in development and review and the willingness to constantly review activities for their effectiveness and to course-correct on a continual basis.

The depth of relationships within a programme, project or team therefore becomes critical, as does the willingness to have bravery and courage in those relationships, to challenge and to embrace constant change. This requires a level of daily resilience in a millennial leader and in the participants that is not commonly found and that needs to be intentionally nurtured and developed.

It also requires the ability to create space for insight and creativity: to be focused on allowing colleagues space to walk, get perspective, be away from the day to day and to absorb different voices and opinions.

Millennial leaders must build multi-disciplinary, diverse teams who have a range of perspectives and who are able to speak and act from a breadth of global and sector experience.

GUT INSTINCT AND EXPERIMENTATION

Rachel: As millennials, we can't quite imagine a world where instant feedback isn't the norm and we are used to getting it direct from the source. One interviewee expressed this as 'we want that engagement straight away'.

Digital technology has brought us closer to colleagues and customers wherever they are in the world and our ability to adapt and experiment has increased dramatically as a result.

Therefore, we are wrestling with the benefits of applying 'test and learn' and 'agile' technologies, and the challenges of the organizational and cultural change that is required as a result.

The speed we expect something to work at and the approach we take to solving a problem is really quite different from that of previous generations and there is a strong desire for greater use of technology in experimentation and problem solving.

Simon: One millennial leader I know, who is Head of Digital in a major corporate, has made it her life mission to enable the senior leadership team to understand how millennials use technology and how they experiment, and to help them change the organizational culture to reflect that. It's a source of constant tension in most organizations I know.

Over the past decade, 'digital transformation' programmes have enabled organizations to increase the level of experimentation involved in marketing and communications programmes, due to the availability of instant feedback.

It is therefore now quite normal for companies to run multiple Facebook advertising campaigns at one time, gauging within minutes the relative success of a particular variant of an advert, measured by engagements, likes, comments and shares, and then to maximize their reach through spending their advertising budget on the winning ads. Similarly, with email marketing campaigns, it's not unusual to have multiple variants of an email with instant feedback available on the number of 'opens', 'reads', 'shares' and 'click-throughs' and on the conversion rate to purchases.

The application of formalized 'test and learn' is growing in popularity outside the digital domain, with new format retail stores being set up as experiments in determining the right formats to drive footfall and revenue growth.

Therefore, the need to pre-determine the exact messaging and make choices has become data-driven and enabled wide experimentation in order to determine the best course of action.

Leaders and managers find themselves creating environments over which they have less control, and in which they can empower their teams to make great choices based on the availability of data and information.

Teams that succeed are collaborative, creative, willing to take risks and to adapt in real time to new information and the changing habits of consumers, and the creation of these agile teams becomes vital to business success.

This requires massive cultural change to be led by millennial leaders. There are some existing, but rare, good models that can help in the process.

While I was in the telecommunications business, I was part of the creation of the Brightstar 'Incubator' to allow us to experiment with new businesses, many of which would fail, and only some of which would succeed. This utilized intellectual property that otherwise would not have been utilized by the business and created new businesses, some of which have been through multiple levels of investment and are successful in their own right today.

Millennial leaders have to be constantly aware of the 'innovator's dilemma'.[13] This has seen the very success of a long-term plan prevent organizations from seizing the opportunity presented by a disruptive technology or market development, because their culture, planning, board make-up and leadership decision-making processes have kept them investing in well-trodden, successful market approaches, while ignoring young startups that will eventually eat them for dinner.

So, the questions, 'Why did the canal owners not become the railway owners? or 'Why did the fixed-line telecoms providers not become the mobile providers?' or 'Why did the hard disk manufacturers not become the solid-state device manufacturers?' haunt company executives and board chairs.

However, as the *Harvard Business Review* comments, 'test and learn' is not always appropriate and millennial leaders need to determine when operating out of a gut instinct based on relevant experience is the most impactful option.

> Generally speaking, the triumphs of testing occur in strategy execution, not strategy formulation. Whether in marketing, store or branch location analysis, or website design, the most reliable insights relate to the potential impact and value of tactical changes: a new store format, for example, or marketing promotion or service process. Scientific method is not well suited to assessing a major change in business models, a large merger or acquisition, or some other game-changing decision.[14]

This is a specific area where older leaders and millennial leaders need to work very closely together to create the right environment to balance the need to experiment with the 'gut feel' that comes from experience, market knowledge and sound strategy formulation. Millennial leaders need to tune themselves in to the 'gut feel' of experience and older leaders need to free themselves up to get closer to their customers through disintermediation and experimentation.

PRIVACY AND TRANSPARENCY

Simon: Undercover reporters, mystery shoppers, CCTV cameras and the proliferation of camera phones mean that there are fewer and fewer places for people to hide. Whatever you think of Julian Assange and of Wikileaks, or of the Freedom of Information Act, or of Google and Amazon and Facebook and other large organizations who capture significant amounts of data about individuals, the balance between privacy and transparency of information has shifted.

In the UK, the government now demands businesses publish information on gender pay gaps, requires the BBC and charities to publish the pay of their most senior executives and publishes league tables of schools and hospitals in order to boost the performance of the worst and encourage competition among the best.

The challenge for millennial leaders is to lead in an environment where data is made more readily available to staff, customers, shareholders and the public and to lead with authenticity within that environment. With trust in large organizations waning over issues such as executive pay, tax avoidance and abuse of power, those that can learn to be more transparent and open with information will win the custom of many doubters.

Rachel: Transparency within an organization is something millennials look for and desire in a place they work at or support. Why give your hard efforts and allegiance to something that isn't able to be transparent and own up to failings?

To millennials, an organization that is guarded and closed shows that it's hiding something and that is not an organization we want to align ourselves with. With more and more scandals within the news of CEOs and companies pulling strings behind closed doors, this attraction to transparency is greater than ever.

Simon: Transparency is a new goal for many businesses, winning over shareholders, employees and the general public. When a business is open about its operations, it can earn a level of trust that it wouldn't have established otherwise.

However, misuse of customers' data can lead to an increase in mistrust between businesses and consumers, as we have seen with the difficulties that Facebook have faced in dealing with the potential misuse of Facebook users' data for political purposes through Cambridge Analytics, which affected 87 million users worldwide and resulted in a significant drop in the organization's share price.

The backlash against this, as people realize that organizations such as Facebook and Google have significant access to data that reveals patterns of behaviour, location, shopping habits, travel schedules and step-counts, is significant.

Similarly, in the charity world, the case of Olive Cooke, a pensioner who received significant levels of unsolicited direct mail through the inappropriate selling of mailing lists and the passing on of donor details from organization to organization, resulted in the formulation of the Fundraising Regulator and dramatic clampdowns in favour of the privacy of individuals.[15]

Companies working in Europe have also had to address their use and storage of data through the implementation of the EU regulations on data usage and storage, known as GDPR.[16]

Supply-chain transparency

For outwear company Patagonia,[17] providing transparency throughout its supply chain means reducing any negative social and environmental impacts the company might have. Many companies have been caught off guard by information about environmentally unfriendly habits of its manufacturers or distributors. So, to prevent this, Patagonia takes a proactive approach, taking the responsibility on itself to make sure no harm is being caused in the making of its products. The project is called 'Footprint Chronicles' and is displayed to the general public through videos on the company's website.

Millennial leaders must push towards new levels of transparency for their companies and new levels of authenticity and integrity for themselves as leaders, while ensuring the privacy of individuals' data and information. It's a tension to be managed and managed well.

WHOLE-HEARTED COMMITMENT AND WHOLE-LIFE FLOURISHING

Rachel: In our research, only eight per cent of millennials said that achieving at work is the priority in our lives (see Figure 2.5).

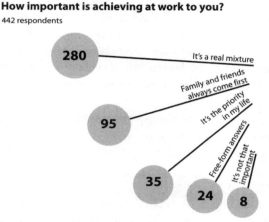

How important is achieving at work to you?
442 respondents

280 — It's a real mixture

95 — Family and friends always come first

35 — It's the priority in my life

24 — Free-form answers

8 — It's not that important

Figure 2.5 The importance of achieving at work

As seen earlier, there is evidence that we have not yet got the balance of work and life right, with over one third of respondents being partly satisfied or not at all satisfied with their work–life balance.

Of major concern is that millennial leaders are facing higher burnout rates than previous generations because of their unique circumstances.[18]

I saw this in our research. One millennial I interviewed, we'll call him Jim, listed 'someone who is burnt out' as one of the worst types of leaders. Yet he also coupled this with saying:

> Lots of my peers have needed counselling over recent years just because of the challenge of just keeping going. So when you ask, 'How do you cope?' I don't think I am fully. When I am leading other community leaders . . . they are just saying, 'Look I'm tired, burnt out, life is hard.'

One surprising result from the research was the love/hate relationship that millennials have with technology. As digital natives, it is part and parcel of our lives and there are areas of our lives that are more difficult and less enjoyable without playlists, instant messaging and Instagram. We also see the amazing potential for business growth and influence through technology.

However, millennials also expressed the emotional drain and pressure that always-on technology can present, with constant updates and the impact of never fully shutting down and resting.

It's a complex and nuanced picture.

In our in-depth interviews, some millennials saw a very clear distinction between work and life and wanted to make sure work did not encroach on their opportunity to 'live' and have time to do what they wanted.

Others, however, saw very blurred lines between work and life, and struggled to balance the boundaries. This was the case especially in jobs within non-corporate agencies such as the caring professions, charities and faith-based organizations, because of the blurred lines between work, personal ministry and friendships.

Here's a selection of what millennials are saying:

> I need to get a better work-life balance because at the moment I am probably 70 per cent living to work and I want that to change so I'm only working to live.

I have always found this work-life balance thing quite a hard thing to grapple with for the reason that I think if you are really passionate about what you do and why you are doing it, then that will overflow.

I've definitely got quite a healthy work-life balance and have a bit of perspective in terms of it's not all about work.

The commitment dilemma

Simon: The spectrum of millennial leaders' views on this subject is not generally well understood by senior leaders. I was recently talking to the CEO of a large organization in the UK. As we explored how he could reposition the organization he led to be relevant to the causes and purposes that millennials were expressing, he opened up about a personnel dilemma he currently faced. A high-performing millennial leader was being seriously considered for promotion in his organization.

The senior team had seen the contribution being made and admired the character and competency of the individual, who was clearly performing at a higher level than this person's peers or anyone comparatively outside the organization.

All was going well until the conversation turned to commitment and comments started to be made about how this individual always left the office at 4.50 p.m. on the nose.

Older leaders began to question this person's commitment to the organization and whether, despite the obvious signs of significant contribution, commitment was lacking.

For the older leaders, this was a major red flag and was blocking the promotion. The CEO was deeply questioning whether this was something that 'we just have to live with from millennials' or whether he should be challenging the millennial towards greater levels of commitment and presence in the office.

It's extremely evident in the day-to-day decisions that businesses are making that they need a new set of glasses to look at this polarity from.

Should businesses adapt their expectations or 'just live with it'?

Rachel: I think 'just live with it' is an unfair phrase to put on millennials. I really understand the importance this millennial places on leaving work at 4.50pm. Maybe she volunteers with a charity after work, has children to care for, friends to meet and support, classes, appointments . . . there are so many reasons.

Surely employees who put time into other areas of life, who are re-energized when they come back to work the next morning because they have attended to all areas of their well-being, are productive and efficient employees? Maybe the focus on thriving with the balance of work and life and not just surviving is something to celebrate and not 'just live with'.

We don't only want career success. The drive for that didn't always lead the previous generation to good places of well-being.

Gallup[19] identified that value and satisfaction for millennials are to be found in work *and* 'life as a whole', not through treating them as two separate activities. The key question for us is not 'What do you do?' but 'Who are you?' This underlying belief causes us to gravitate towards businesses that are ethically conscious and good corporate citizens, finding those businesses attractive to work in.

You see, millennials are committed. We are wholly committed to work when we are working, but we want to be wholly committed to friends, wholly committed to family, to our health and to our well-being alongside that.

Simon: The challenge for millennial leaders is to maximize the level of commitment that millennials bring and their focus on making a difference and aligning with purpose, while at the same time creating environments in which millennials can achieve a great whole-life balance.

Lead employers, such as Price Waterhouse Coopers (PWC), have been the first to adapt to these changes by introducing a range of flexible working practices with ten per cent of employees worldwide being on reduced hours. They also offer the opportunity of working flexible hours in flexible locations and have introduced a company-wide education programme for older leaders to educate them on how millennials are leading differently.

Bob Moritz, the Chairman of PWC in the USA, comments:

Millennials are less willing than Boomers to make their work lives an exclusive priority, even when offered the prospect of substantial future compensation. They want job flexibility in the here and now, along with opportunities for training and mobility and better and more frequent feedback and rewards . . . What has changed is the definition of commitment. It no longer encompasses sacrificing health or throwing work/life flexibility out of whack, but it still includes what really matters for business outcomes: a devotion to the missions of the client and the firm.[20]

SAFETY AND CHALLENGE

Simon: There is an increasing realization that the well-being of individuals in the workplace is a critical issue for millennial leaders, and that the foundational issue is creating an environment in which employees feel safe: physiologically, physically and psychologically safe.

Anyone who has even briefly looked at Maslow's hierarchy of needs will not find this to be a surprise; the bottom two layers being the meeting of physiological needs and the need for safety. Without these in place, the ability to experience love, belonging, self-esteem and self-actualization in the individual is, according to Maslow, impossible.

In a corporate or community sense, the ability for employees to feel part of a community, to take risks, be creative, reach their full potential, rise to challenges and align with the purpose of an organization, requires first of all physiological safety.

Physiological
How can I prosper at work and make a maximum contribution if my physical needs are not being met? If I am worrying about how my family will be fed tonight? Or have unreliable tools?

Physical
A physically safe workplace is not just about being free from injury there, but also being free from sickness and disease. It means an environment that is physically safe for everyone who works there and includes addressing issues such as staff well-being and lone working.

Employees who perceive the workplace as protective of physical safety will also feel more secure and engaged at work, with increased mental and physical well-being.

Psychological

Everyone has mental health, just like everyone has physical health. There has been increasing awareness of the negative impact that destructive, dysfunctional teams and relationships can have on the mental health of employees. No one wants to go to work in an environment that is stressful, relationally poor, disrespectful and emotionally and mentally draining.

Rachel: Millennial leaders are no longer willing to accept that as a reasonable or sustainable workplace environment. How safe is your workplace and how safe is your leadership?

These are vital questions for millennial leaders as, without safety in the workplace, employees cannot thrive under your leadership and will not be willing to take risks, be the best creative person they can possibly be and be challenged to increase their performance and deliver even greater business benefit.

The purpose of initiatives that create safety is not to pander to an 'entitled' millennial generation, or to regard millennials as 'snowflakes' who need wrapping in cotton wool and to have their egos massaged. They are fundamentally good for business.

Their purpose is rather to create an environment that allows people to bring the whole of themselves to work, enabling them to focus not on what could or will harm them, but on what will and can grow their careers, grow their personality, grow their influence and grow their business.

As Simon Sinek says in his TED Talk, 'Why good leaders make you feel safe':

> When a leader makes the choice to put the safety and lives of the people inside the organization first, to sacrifice their comforts and

sacrifice the tangible results, so that the people remain and feel safe and feel like they belong, remarkable things happen . . . We call them leaders because they take the risk before anybody else does. We call them leaders because they will choose to sacrifice so that their people may be safe and protected and so their people may gain, and when we do, the natural response is that our people will sacrifice for us. They will give us their blood and sweat and tears to see that their leader's vision comes to life, and when we ask them, 'Why would you do that? Why would you give your blood and sweat and tears for that person?' they all say the same thing: 'Because they would have done it for me.' And isn't that the organization we would all like to work in?[21]

This is a challenge worth aspiring to.

THIS NEW ENVIRONMENT REQUIRES A DIFFERENT TYPE OF LEADERSHIP APPROACH

Simon: Great windsurfers immediately recognize when wind conditions have changed (wind direction, speed etc.), so their position and approach can quickly adapt in response. They have learnt to read the changes in the environment. The same is true of great leaders.

I remember walking into my director's office early in my career at about 10.30 a.m. He was sitting, drinking coffee and reading the *Financial Times*. He saw my bewildered look as I had been hard at work delivering since 7 a.m., and sought to explain:

You see, Simon, very few people understand that my job as a leader is not to deliver the status quo. It's to understand the environment in which we are working, to sense the changes and then to assist my team in navigating the changes we need to make to thrive in that new environment.

One of the most important skills for a millennial leader is scanning the environment, sensing the changes and then processing the data quickly, adapting strategy and maximizing effectiveness in the new environment.

Drawing on all our work and research on the environment in which millennial leaders operate, we have identified the top 20 leadership approaches that have to change within this new environment (see Table 2.1). We have tested these on many leaders (millennials and non-millennials) and have found that everyone has a mix of approaches, using some tools that once worked and are now less effective and others that are highly effective now. Which ones would you tick as your current approach?

Table 2.1 The top 20 leadership approaches, past and present

	What has worked previously	*What works now*
1	Lead from what you do	Lead from who you are
2	Create environments where you win	Create environments where everyone wins
3	Celebrate the individual	Celebrate the team
4	Win at work/lose at home	Win everywhere
5	Create a flexible environment	Develop a sense of community
6	Business is good for the shareholders	Business is good for employees, community and shareholders

(continued)

Table 2.1 (*continued*)

	What has worked previously	*What works now*
7	Total commitment to work	Total commitment to life
8	Lead from the top down	Lead from anywhere
9	Use data to prove everything and create a grand plan	Go with your gut and experiment
10	Good ideas come from a small number of people	Good ideas can come from anywhere and anyone
11	A job is for life – you need to have a career	Flexibility, moving around, getting great experience of work and life
12	Feedback on performance from one person, once a year	Feedback on performance from anyone at any time
13	Business is a series of transactions	Business is a series of relationships
14	The end justifies the means	Integrity is everything
15	Leadership is power	Leadership is service
16	Winning in the short term	Winning for the long term
17	Developing people is a waste of time because they move on	We need to develop the next generation now, so that everyone wins
18	Drive people with targets	Inspire people with purpose
19	Leaders need to be guarded and measured	Leaders need to be open and vulnerable and transparent
20	The winner has the greatest market share this year	The winner is still here when we are all gone

Rachel: As millennials, we recognize the change and the conflict in the environment. However, from our interviews, it was clear that we are often frustrated by our own organizations not keeping up with the pace of change. For example, we are seeing such fast advances in the world of technology, yet one millennial shared with me that her organization is 'still quite backwards in terms of how we do things' and that she is 'trying to move forward', while another frustratedly expressed that her organization 'is about 30 years behind'.

We need and desire leaders who will grasp this change, those who will quickly process, adapt and configure themselves and this new environment to maximize effectiveness in it.

WHAT DOES THIS ALL MEAN?

Rachel: In Part two, we will show how millennials have been poorly stereotyped and how, underlying those stereotypes, are strong, core beliefs that provide a solid foundation on which millennial leaders can build. Leading out of these core beliefs, we will see how millennials are already making a significant difference as leaders in this new environment and are instrumental in driving many of the changes we are seeing. However, the opportunities for the millennial generation's true and full contribution to the world are still to be revealed.

Also in Part two, we will show where the gaps in the millennial's armour are and how we can develop the tools to address the tensions expressed in the research and find a depth of character and maturity, focus, energy and resilience to make the most of this opportunity. The question is, will we grasp this moment?

Part two

MARKS OF THE MILLENNIAL LEADER

INTRODUCTION TO PART TWO

Simon: The Karamajong are a little known tribe in the north west of Uganda. Unlike their cousins the Masai, who have been on the tourist itinerary for decades, very few people visit the Karamajong, who live in the poorest and most marginalized part of the country.

I had the privilege of travelling to Karamoja in 2010 where we were undertaking a three-year programme to improve maternal child health in an area where only one in five children reach the age of five.

On any visit to the Karamajong, it doesn't take long to realize that they are characterized by three things:

First, by the manyattas in which the sub-groups of each tribe live. These are circular compounds that are visible as you fly into the local airport and mark the extent of an extended family's community.

The second characteristic is their high regard for cattle, which they believe have been given to them by their God AKUJ. AKUJ also gifted them the cattle of their neighbouring tribes (while not telling the neighbouring tribes about it!).

The third characteristic is that, because of famine and malnutrition in the region, they have been fed by the United Nations World

Food Programme for over 40 years and therefore have developed a dependency culture.

These are the outward marks of the Karamajong leaders and reflect their inner values and beliefs that have been formed over centuries, defining how they interact with the world.

Some of these attributes are strong and healthy and some require development and change.

What are the marks of the millennial leader? Which ones are inherent and strong and which need development? Let's explore this together.

Chapter three

HOW AND WHY YOU HAVE BEEN MISUNDERSTOOD

Rachel: Historically, generations have always been categorized, labelled and scrutinized. Labelled 'millennials', we are no different, with large amounts of research and literature focusing on who we are, our characteristics and how we make an impact on society.

In fact, it is claimed that millennial professionals 'are one of the most discussed and researched subjects of recent time'.[1]

Maybe this is just a coming of age thing, because there is no doubt that millennials are now young adults and we constitute a major section of the workforce and occupy many leadership roles.[2]

Simon: A detailed scan of all the research and articles sees millennials being categorized and generalized by academics, social commentators and millennials themselves.

Hobart and Sendek in their book, *Gen Y Now*, identify from their research seven 'myths' or consistent stereotypes that millennials have been labelled with:

1 lazy/slacker
2 instant gratification and wanting a trophy for showing up
3 self-centred/narcissistic
4 disloyal
5 pampered/spoilt
6 lack of respect for authority
7 entitled.

They go on to argue that these stereotypes are either 'misconceptions and exaggerations or they are traits that can actually lead to positive and productive Gen Y (millennial) performance in the workplace'.[3]

Rachel and I agree with them and believe that millennials have been over-stereotyped and poorly caricatured and, based on Hobart and Sendek's work in exploding these myths,[4] our own more recent research argues for a much more nuanced view.

Underneath the stereotypes, our research has identified really strong and positive core beliefs that need to be understood. These strong beliefs, if harnessed by the millennial leader for positive momentum, the way windsurfers do with strong winds, could turn the world of work upside down in a positive way. Conversely, if they are continually misread, they have substantial potential to rip businesses and organizations apart and to throw windsurfers into the deep.

This is 'conflict central', the battleground of beliefs and approaches that is causing us all so much grief.

As Hobart and Sendek so brilliantly put it, 'Different too often equals wrong. As a leader your job is to recognize that different equals different . . . and then lead your troops to that same understanding.'[5]

We must put down any prejudices and enter conflict central, being willing to imagine a collaborative future.

MILLENNIAL STEREOTYPES

Stereotype 1: lazy/slacker
Simon: The stereotype of lazy/slacker is commonplace and often used when older leaders see millennials leaving work consistently on

time or arriving late or not 'putting in the extra hours'. What is being observed here is an outward expression of a deeply held core belief.

Core belief: the whole of life matters

Rachel: We found from our research that there was definitely a change in the nature of commitment to work among millennials and that this is being driven by a core positive belief that the whole of life matters.

We believe that employers need to grasp this change in the nature of commitment and to build on the positive core belief in millennials towards a commitment to the whole of life. So, when an employee leaves on time, they shouldn't be viewed as being lazy or a slacker but as someone who has a commitment to being fully productive, fully alive and fully committed to work while at work and fully alive outside work as well.

Positive contribution: productive/fully alive

Simon: If businesses can tap into this core belief, then the positive contribution could increase workplace productivity across all generations.

It's a journey I've been on myself. How productive am I actually if I don't take proper rest and don't balance my life? A report in *The Economist*, for example, quotes a study showing that output at 70 hours a week is the same as at 56 hours a week, resulting in 14 wasted hours in terms of productivity.[6]

One of the millennials we interviewed told us the story of how, at her final interview for her graduate scheme at a major corporate, she asked whether, if they employed her, she could take a year off before joining to travel the world. They agreed and, after three months of induction, she left to follow her dreams, returning nine months later.

This enlightened employer saw the huge value of their new employee bringing the diversity and depth of her experience to the workplace, the benefit of her being fully engaged and the value of that employee's whole life being enriched.

Stereotype 2: instant gratification

Millennials have been stereotyped as wanting instant gratification, as not being prepared to wait for anything and as being impatient for change, acknowledgment and promotion.

Many of my peers are shocked at graduates leaving their firms after one or two years because they didn't get the promotion they thought they deserved.

Rachel: Our research showed that millennials are constantly comparing their performance with others and that we are used to the world constantly changing and evolving and having to evolve rapidly with it. As we are used to rapid progress, we tend to have frustrations with anything that takes time or maturity or that needs patience.

Core belief: expect rapid results

Simon: Millennials have grown up expecting rapid results. They are used to instant feedback on every performance and to being judged on results only and not on age or longevity of service.

Underlying this is the core belief that they can adapt quickly, grow rapidly and continually learn.

To counter instant gratification and deal with failure, rapid and real feedback can significantly help millennials to be mentored through the need for patience and application in achieving long-term impact as well as rapid results.

Positive contribution: fast and adaptive

The positive contribution is that millennial leaders are incredibly adaptive to change and fast to react to evolving situations, a set of attributes that, when highly valued and channelled, can make for a significant competitive advantage.

Stereotype 3: narcissistic

Rachel: Self-centred and narcissistic is one of the most common stereotypes I hear thrown at us. There is no doubt that some millennials have grown up in a world where their parents' self-worth has been bound up in their children's achievement. I know that's not true of all of us, and it hasn't been my experience, but I still recognize this and have seen many examples of it.

This, coupled with the huge choice and diversity available to us and a greater degree of awareness of all the options out there, can lead to a perception that we are self-obsessed, believing the world revolves around us and our happiness.

This was definitely a significant tension in the research as we saw ourselves wrestling with our own identity, our self-confidence and our self-esteem, while also believing that individually and corporately we have the skills, knowledge and aptitude to bring a new creativity and fresh innovation to the world.

Core belief: I am enough

Simon: I think that, in reality, every generation going through early adulthood experiences the challenge of wrestling with self-identity, self-confidence and self-esteem, and millennials seem to be wrestling with this more than most.

There is a huge commitment though to the core beliefs that each person is enough, each person is valued, each person has a unique contribution to make and each person needs to come to the full expression of their whole self.

Although we may not have seen this yet in its fullness, the world of business will benefit greatly from its ripening and the richness and diversity it can bring.

Positive contribution: personal reputation

A positive contribution of these core beliefs that we observed in the research, is that millennial leaders are passionate about reputation, image and personal brand and therefore want to be seen to be doing a good job. They want the organizations that they are working for to look good and have a positive image and they want to be positive representations of that brand in the marketplace.

Stereotype 4: disloyal

A good friend of mine runs a national charity that recruits many graduates. He recounted to me a story of a recent round table with several of their graduate recruits. One of them, let's call him Tom, started to explain how committed he was to the organization. He said:

> You know that I am so committed to the purpose of this organization. I want you to know that I'm so thrilled to have this position and I so believe in what you are doing that I have determined not to start looking for anything else outside the organization for at least a year.

You may resonate with the way Tom is thinking, but it does throw out some real challenges. Even though the desire for purpose is very strong in millennial leaders (our research showed that 86 per cent of millennials thought it was extremely or very important that the purpose of the organization matched their sense of purpose), there is still the sense that this is more about 'me' than it is about the organization and that a sense of duty is missing (hence the 'disloyalty' tag).

Core belief: purpose really matters

Rachel: Purpose is the big factor for me in choosing a job. In fact, I can only really be happy to take a job I find a lack of purpose in if I have a strong sense of purpose in another area of my life. For example, I worked in a supermarket for a season. For me, it was boring and lacked purpose but, in a sense, I also had purpose in it: to earn enough to go to Canada for five months on a leadership course.

So, while I stacked shelves and dealt with yet another grumpy customer, I had a greater sense of purpose and vision in where this was going to take me. There's certainly a search for purpose and meaning whether it's in or out of my job.

In my experience, other millennials and organizations are becoming more aware that a job is likely to be temporary and on the path to a greater purpose, than the lifetime career that older generations would have settled into.

For me, it's a much more fulfilling and exciting way to live. I would be much more likely to stay in a job with purpose for longer than one where I found the purpose more difficult to see.

Positive contribution: purposeful

Simon: For organizations, this is a massive challenge and requires a changed mindset that asks the question, 'How do we benefit most from aligning a millennial's purpose and productivity for the time he or she is with us?', rather than, 'How do we retain this employee for the longest time possible?'.

This can be facilitated by enabling millennials to help the organization develop a shared sense of purpose, which we will explore later.

Stereotype 5: pampered/spoilt

Predominantly, this egocentric streak is attributed to millennials' upbringing.

Raised when strict discipline was giving way to fashionable attachment parenting, which eschewed routine and rules and tended to a child's needs on demand, there is no doubt that some millennials were pampered and indeed some may even have been spoilt. But to stereotype a whole generation with these words is, we believe, mistaken.

From an early age, many millennials were certainly taught to put themselves first. Middle-class millennials were the beneficiaries of baby boomer parents with dual incomes, in the midst of a period of unprecedented economic growth and opportunity.

However, that quickly turned into recession and loss just as millennials were coming of age, and the challenges of finding graduate jobs in the middle of a recession speedily led to a passion for fair play and justice – for everyone.

Core belief: fair play and justice

Rachel: I see many of those we interviewed in the research really understanding the privilege of the upbringings they have had and wanting to turn that to the advantage of everyone. Therefore, I listened to many who are giving up holidays and spare time to volunteer in food banks, with survivors of trafficking, in homeless shelters and are running marathons to raise money for charity. There was a definite sense that we want to see fair play and justice.

Positive contribution: growing self-confidence
Simon: The supportive and encouraging environment that millennials have been brought up in, combined with their access to knowledge, information and education, has definitely also led to a self-confidence that appears on the surface to be ahead of their years and their experience. However, our research has also shown that this self-confidence does have a sensitive underside and can easily be knocked by negative feedback or criticism, which taps into the entitled/pampered/spoilt stereotype. This can easily affect self-esteem.

As millennial leaders take up increasingly senior positions, there is a need to bring together the sense of fair play and justice with a stronger core that assists millennials in developing greater resilience to conflict and feedback, and helps them to wrestle with ensuring that their self-confidence comes out of a fuller picture of themselves and their identity.

Stereotype 6: lack of respect for authority
One of the biggest challenges to the harmony of the workplace is the perception that millennials have a disrespect for authority.

A friend who has been a business leader for over 35 years recently told me of a situation in their business where a young intern was making a habit of consistently criticizing the leader's performance at the weekly team meeting on a Monday morning.

His critique was about the irrelevance of the business strategy to the culture in which he was living and working. However, the staff team were horrified that the intern would even dare to speak, given his lack of experience of business or leadership, and saw this as disrespect.

We have all experienced similar situations and it requires leaders of great character and with high levels of security in their identity to enable an environment in which feedback like this can be given and received with grace and humility.

Core belief: authenticity
Rachel: Montes[7] warns those in authority not to take millennials' confrontational style or questioning as rude, but as a way of understanding and processing information and driving for authenticity.

Millennials have grown up seeing the failures, both moral and functional, of businesses, political parties, governments, families, faith groups and communities. We know the hypocrisy and double-speaking that has characterized many leaders' lives over many decades.

In our research, integrity, authenticity and humility are at the tops of our 'must have' lists in leaders we want to work for. Millennials will therefore not blindly follow an institution or leader, but will want to research information themselves too, enabled by access to extensive knowledge through technology.

Positive contributions: curiosity/integrity
Simon: The major positive contributions that millennials can bring are in encouraging much greater openness and honesty in the workplace, enabling people to be more real and to face up to significant issues and creating a culture that prizes curiosity, feedback, learning and development.

If those are the values and culture that a leader, a business or organization wants to develop, then employing millennials to enable you to do that and to be formative in their creation would be a great way forward.

Stereotype 7: entitled

From being entitled to a place at university to being entitled to a job and success, millennials have been promised the world and are expectant that they can grab it with both hands.

Core belief: a desire to be successful

Rachel: By and large, we have the optimism and self-confidence to be able to grasp opportunity and the desire to be successful. We also have more access to experience and knowledge than any generation before us to enable us to achieve success.

However, as in every generation before us, we are learning that it sounds much easier than it actually is in practice.

Positive contribution: perseverance

In the Forge Leadership research, millennials felt optimistic about the future and not disillusioned by early failures and challenges.

Millennials have a high degree of self-confidence, the determination to succeed and the energy, hope and vision to persevere and overcome some of the significant barriers that have been put in our way.

Throughout university, I had planned to do a graduate scheme afterwards that would have involved me moving to a new city and working in the sector I wanted to be in. I made decisions based on this and was prepared with experience and skills I thought would suit the position, yet about six months before the planned start, I got a call. I was told that, following the selection day I had attended a few weeks previously, I had not been selected. This knocked my confidence and stability because the plans I had made no longer made sense and questions of whether I would be good enough to apply for other schemes or jobs surfaced in my head.

However, I made a decision after that phone call to persevere. I chose to build my resilience and look for the next thing, which actually ended up being a lot more suited to me and much more exciting than I had thought!

Table 3.1 provides a summary of millennial stereotypes and the beliefs and contributions that underlie them.

Table 3.1 Summary of millennial stereotypes

Stereotype	Core beliefs	Positive contribution
Lazy/slacker	The whole of life matters	Productive/fully alive
Instant gratification	Expect rapid results	Fast and adaptive
Narcissistic	I am enough	Innovative/creative/diverse
Disloyal	Purpose really matters	Purposeful/life-long learners
Pampered/spoilt	Fair play and justice	Growing self-confidence
Lack of respect for authority	Authenticity	Curious/authentic
Entitled	A desire to be successful	Persevering

One of the interviewees in our research summed this all up well, with the following statement:

> So, I always laugh about the lazy, entitled, narcissistic piece because actually I think they are pretty good labels.

We are lazy so that means we are going to find the most efficient way to get something done, and find me an organization who doesn't want the most efficient way.

We are entitled, which means we think we will get this stuff, so we'll find a way to make it happen. We will work at it until it changes. And we are narcissistic, so we want it to look good and feel good.

Tell me an organization that doesn't want to enjoy products that feel good, look good and are the best they can be.

They are actually really positive contributions for what we think is best.

Chapter four

INTRODUCING THE FIVE 'I'S OF LEADERSHIP

Rachel: For us, one of our interviewees, we will call her Megan, exemplified the type of leader that a millennial is:

Megan was the CEO of an anti-trafficking charity for three years and has since co-founded a natural foods and drinks company existing to provide training and employment for survivors of trafficking. She also works as a freelance leadership development consultant, coaching and facilitating leaders from a wide variety of sectors, businesses and NGOs.

Megan remembers creating her own 'care clubs' when she was eight, perhaps the early signs of her sense of purpose revolving around helping people become the best they can be. That led her to a graduate scheme with a large food company and eventually into her career in leadership development.

Then, in 2015 while on a retreat in California, Megan felt the call to play a role in helping women who are survivors of trafficking and to pursue a future focused on building networks of 'women supporting women' and 'businesses supporting women'.

Megan describes what happened next:

> I returned from the retreat into a really exciting role that had Europe-wide responsibilities. However, I quickly ended up quite burnt out (down, of course, to my own proving tendencies!). I remember doing 17 flights in three weeks. After a couple of

months of this, I decided to move to London, partly to be nearer the airports and partly to do something in the charity sector.

Then, when I arrived in London, the company ended up reducing travel allowances and I started working from home. I went from deep and authentic community to almost complete isolation, loneliness and confusion. It was at that point that I realized perhaps the purpose and vision I had received while away in California might be for now. I couldn't shake the deep conviction that I was meant to leave my job to take a step into pursuing that vision.

It was from that challenge and pain that I got the courage to make the biggest leadership decision of my life so far, which was to leave my job.

When I resigned I had nothing to go to, which was unheard of! But I left with a final email out to my stakeholders telling them I was leaving to set up an employability programme for survivors of trafficking. And just two weeks later, I was offered a role to lead a small anti-trafficking charity, without even applying for it! And along the journey, I was blessed to be invested in and trusted by some consultancies I had met, who gave me opportunities to do consulting work, making the move to start working for the charity financially feasible.

So, from that, an employability programme was started. Many safe-house providers report concerns about the long-term safety and reintegration of survivors of trafficking, with many fearing that high numbers of survivors are then re-trafficked because they are still vulnerable to traffickers, homelessness and poverty.

I found some friends who shared the same passion and together we started these programmes as a comprehensive programme of workshops, placements, coaching and accessing training or formal learning, designed to support survivors as they transition from emergency care.

The transformation we saw in women's lives is quite remarkable and humbling.

Megan continues:

Anyone is a leader if they believe they can make a positive difference in the world and have a positive impact on people around them. It's about looking outside yourself.

I truly believe that everyone has leadership within them, and more often than not it comes from having a deep sense of purpose, knowing why you exist and taking steps to move towards that.

I think if you put a group in a room, your natural leaders will emerge whether there are titles or not, because there's something within them that will say, 'I want to have an impact on this group, to make some kind of change and have an influence of some kind.'

For me, having an intention, then following it through to bring others with you in any given circumstance makes someone a leader. I think it's the heart of leadership.

WHAT'S MISSING?

Simon: We return to the question of what kind of leaders millennials will be.

How can you build on your core beliefs to effectively lead in today's business environment?

It is our argument that the core beliefs of millennial leaders that we have explored, have uniquely positioned them for exactly this task and they are already achieving extraordinary results, like Megan.

It would be easy to stop at this point and say 'job done'. Just lean into your core beliefs and you're sorted. Just be you and all will be fine.

If only it was that easy!

THE CHALLENGES IN THE RESEARCH

Simon: In the Forge Leadership research there were five challenges that stood out and really made us think.

1 Millennial leaders want to be secure in their **identity** but are really wrestling with their **need for approval**.
2 Millennial leaders want to lead with **integrity** but are wrestling with the **fear of failure**.
3 Millennial leaders want to be **fully alive** yet are wrestling with how to have the mental, physical, emotional and spiritual **inner strength**.
4 Millennial leaders want to create space for **insight** and creativity, but are wrestling with **whole-life balance** and blurred boundaries.
5 Millennial leaders have a strong desire to **influence** and make a difference but are wrestling with **how to do that well**.

At Forge Leadership we have therefore developed a set of five leadership key attributes that build on millennial leaders' existing core beliefs.

They will enable you to wrestle with these polarities, the way windsurfers wrestle with the tension in the wind and the waves, and to create a leadership posture that strengthens your core and enables you to stay the course, to maximize your potential energy and to accelerate your momentum as you ride the biggest waves of your career.

These key attributes comprise five 'I's that will establish or enhance you as a millennial leader others will want to follow; five 'I's that will enable you to lead in a millennial way (see Figure 4.1):

- Identity
- Integrity
- Inner strength
- Insight
- Influence.

The following chapters explore each of these in more detail.

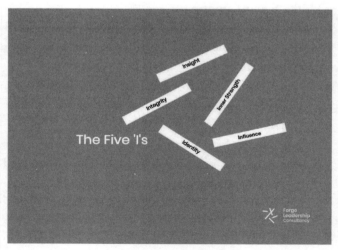

Figure 4.1 Forge Leadership's five leadership key attributes

Chapter five

IDENTITY – IT'S NOT WHO YOU KNOW, IT'S WHO YOU *ARE*

Mark 1: Millennial leaders are secure in their identity, have dealt with their fears, have learnt to be vulnerable and lead out of who they are.

Simon: Who are you when nobody is looking? When your gifts, hobbies, skills, relationships, work, likes and dislikes have been stripped away? What is left?

When asked, 'What are the most important characteristics in the best leaders you have seen?' a large proportion of our interviewees answered with two words: authenticity and integrity. There was real frustration with leaders who publicly come across as having it all together, yet in private their lives and actions do not match up. This was voiced by millennials exclaiming, 'The worst characteristics of a leader that I've known: dishonesty, lack of integrity.'

Integrity and authenticity assume you already know who you are, with the outward display of your actions matching your true identity. Even though the majority of the millennial generation has identified this as key to its leadership, and acts instinctively from a position of wanting to be the same person in work, at home and socially, it may be surprising that many struggle to live from who they are day to day, and wrestle with achieving consistency in how they act in a variety of circumstances.

For example, 60 per cent of millennials recognized that their identity is deeply affected by their performance as leaders and 47 per cent of millennial leaders said their performance at work affects their self-esteem 'a lot' (see Figure 5.1). These struggles put huge pressures on sense of identity and can lead to behaviour that is driven by seeking approval and affirmation of achievement rather than being authentically who we are.

How much does your performance at work affect your self-esteem?
442 respondents

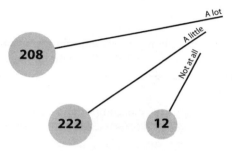

Figure 5.1 How much self-esteem is affected by performance at work

In addition, the 'need for approval' and the 'fear of failure' were most often cited when respondents were asked what would trip them up as leaders (see Figure 5.2). These were listed much higher than pride, sexual temptation, mishandling money or power.

Both these potential hazards indicate the fragility of being consistently our true selves and leading from a position rooted in a secure identity.

How, then, can millennial leaders make sure that they know who they are, that their actions are authentic, that they are worth following?

What are the things that are most likely to have a negative impact on your leadership? Please choose up to 3 that are most relevant.

442 respondents

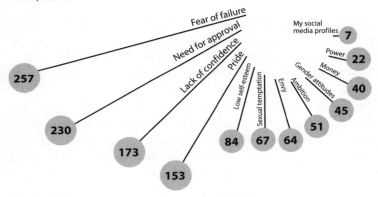

Figure 5.2 Negative impacts on leadership

THE SHIFT: WHY FINDING IDENTITY IS SO VITAL TO MILLENNIAL LEADERS

Simon: I recently watched the Marvel film, *The Avengers: Infinity War*. It's standard comic-strip stuff with a plethora of superheroes from Iron Man to Dr Strange, all trying to save the day. One of the most striking elements of the film for me, though, was the way that the superheroes displayed their humanity and made themselves vulnerable, at one point even talking about the need to lose weight and the brokenness in their families. It may or may not have struck you too? I suppose for me their vulnerability stood at odds with the superheroes I grew up with, who were all brave and courageous, and I (along with many of my generation) felt that, in order to be strong, we had to be the same.

In wanting to be a leader people could follow, many of us fell into the trap of keeping up the superhero act of old, never showing weakness or vulnerability. In reality, in lying to or misleading others as to what we were truly feeling and experiencing, we created many environments of blame, mistrust, power play and threats.

Despite the millennials' desire for wanting to bring their whole selves to every part of their lives, there is much to learn from the struggle the generation before had in starting to break the stereotype of what it means to be a strong leader.

For me, people started identifying leadership as a core skill in my life way before I did. Through their encouragement I went on to do things I never would have dreamed of, such as putting on a whole musical in my late teens, complete with orchestra, choir, actors, ticket sales and rapturous reviews.

Following numerous leadership roles during my education, I ended up in my first job, surrounded by bosses who took risks with me and threw me into positions that would stretch me. And stretch me they did. Returning to work in telecommunications after a secondment to the Cabinet Office in Whitehall, I was put on a fast-track Directors' scheme for the FTSE 100 company. Little did I know that the two-day career counselling course they sent me on would prove the real challenge! There, I was confronted with some cold, hard truths.

First, I was pushing myself so hard to climb the corporate ladder that the people I really loved and cared for were hurting. Second, my motivation for succeeding was really a lack of affirmation in my life and I was seeking this primarily from my work and my bosses. Third, I was prepared to sacrifice my own convictions for my own progression and was now in danger of living a double life and wearing a mask.

Some people can maintain this well, others less so. The whole-life pursuit the millennial generation seeks to encapsulate has been hard won by some of my generation, who have surrendered an old style of leadership in favour of a more integrated approach.

Karen Blackett OBE, Chairwoman of MediaCom, one of the world's largest media and advertising organizations, in an interview with *Director Magazine*, published by the UK Institute of Directors said, 'The leaders who are inspirational to me are who they are. They aren't pretending they have all the answers. They show vulnerability as well as courage.' She goes on to cite a 2014 Deloitte study that shows that 61 per cent of employees cover up their true identities at work in some way. Therefore, Blackett believes that she has to encourage her employees to be themselves at work and says: 'I talk a lot about being able to bring your whole self to work.'[1]

WHY MILLENNIAL LEADERS PLAY A KEY ROLE IN DRIVING THE CHANGE

Rachel: As millennials, we can often take our ability to bring more of our identity to work for granted. However, if we are to overcome the challenges many of us recognized in the research (the fear of failure, the need for approval and to detach our work and self-esteem from our leadership performance), then perhaps the greatest gift we can give our followers is to be more self-aware; more self-intelligent.

'Self-intelligence' is the ability to understand the whole of yourself, that is your gifts, emotions, personality, values and beliefs, and to act out of that understanding with increased 'emotional intelligence' and 'conversational intelligence'. The psychologists Joseph Luft and Harrington Ingham created the 'Johari Window' (see Figure 5.3 overleaf) as a heuristic tool to enable individuals to come to a greater level of understanding of their relationship with themselves and others.[2]

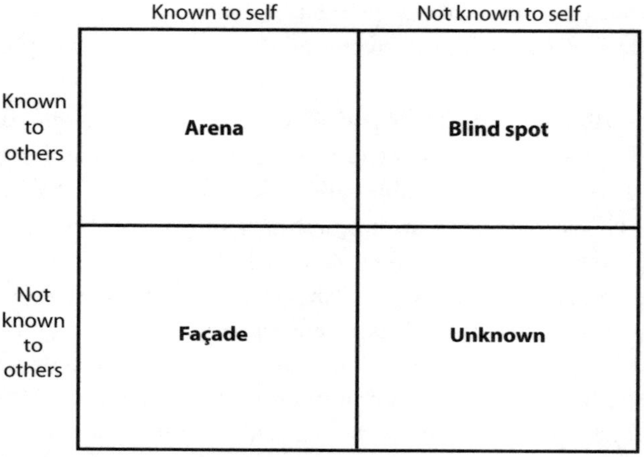

	Known to self	Not known to self
Known to others	**Arena**	**Blind spot**
Not known to others	**Façade**	**Unknown**

Figure 5.3 Johari Window

In this model, the top left quadrant is the known self. This is the area that is public: the 'arena' that is known to self and known to others. It's the arena that we live in every day and is our known 'normal'.

But it's important to go much further than this. And the first area to look at is the things that others know about us and that are obvious to them, but are totally unknown to us. They are our blind spots. The Achilles' heel of every leader; the things that everyone starts talking about as soon as we leave the room, but to which we are completely oblivious.

The second area is the things we know about ourselves but which are invisible to others: the secrets we keep, the revelations of our true selves that need courage and bravery to, as Brené Brown puts it, 'step out . . . and brave the wild'.[3] These are the parts that, when revealed, allow us to bring our whole selves, vulnerably and authentically to the table. Revealing the true me, when the façade is removed, the mask thrown off and the whole of my creative, broken, imperfect and 'glorious self' now visible.

And the final area is the most exciting: the parts of ourselves that we don't know yet and that others don't know either. The parts of our lives that we are exploring and adventuring into with others, learning about ourselves as we try new hobbies, new foods, new activities, new cultures, new jobs and new relationships.

The Johari Window, though created in 1955, is still not as widely applied as it needs to be and can be a helpful tool for the millennial leading today. Tackling our blind spots, getting real and authentic feedback and learning to be vulnerable are core components to overcoming fear and dealing with the need for approval.

DEALING WITH INSECURITY

Simon: For the 47 per cent of millennials whose self-esteem has been tied up in their leadership performance, it can feel as though you've become a prisoner to performing, perfecting and pleasing. This is a key indicator of a lack of security in your identity.

In my experience, every leader of every generation has to face up to insecurity. Constantly and continually. It's a lifelong battle that is never quite won. It's like peeling back the skin of an onion one layer at a time; one fear at a time.

With leaders of all generations, there are five core fears underlying this feeling of being insecure that come up again and again.

Each one on its own is explosive, and combined, they cause most of the drama that we find in organizations today. As John Maxwell has written: 'Insecure leaders are like fireworks with a lit fuse. It's only a matter of time until they explode, and when they do, they hurt everyone close to them.'[4]

The five core fears are

- not being liked
- failure
- rejection
- being found out (impostor syndrome)
- losing power.

Fear of not being liked

One of the most concerning results from our survey was our interviewees' overwhelming desire to be liked by the people they are leading. This is not unique to millennials. Of itself, wanting to be liked is not a bad thing, but when it becomes a fear and therefore a drive to seek approval, a very negative cycle ensues. Once again, the lessons of the past can offer help for today.

I've led managers and leaders for whom, especially early in their careers, this is characteristic of their leadership. Often it can happen when a leader is promoted within his or her own team and given responsibilities for people who once were peers and are now direct reports. The leader now tries to create an environment in which everyone is happy and to maintain existing peer relationships. We all need approval, to feel that we are loved and accepted. However, if our *primary* source of approval comes from the people who are working for us then the behaviours that result become erratic.

There is an explosion waiting to happen. The first time you need to discipline someone, but fail to do so, the first time you have to make a promotion decision, the first time you need to lead the team in a difficult choice – these all provide opportunities for the lit fuse to explode.

Ironically, the result of living out of this fear of lack of approval is a lack of approval. People's respect for you diminishes as they see the inconsistencies of your actions.

Leaders who overcome this fear are able to lead from a secure base of values and beliefs, to articulate them clearly and to act consistently. Millennial leaders see this very clearly as indicated by their high ratings of integrity and strength of character when asked what they looked for in a leader.

Fear of failure

A key indicator that a number of the millennial generation are feeling insecure in their leadership is the high score that our research gave to 'fear of failure' when they were asked what elements would impact their leadership. This would suggest that, for these interviewees, they may not be working in environments of grace and trust where they feel free to make mistakes and learn from them. The best organizations and leaders are actively tackling this by seeking to create environments where leaders can experiment, where it is safe to take measured risks and leaders are given time to come good.

The negative impacts of either leaders or those they are leading not feeling safe to fail is a reduced creativity, an unwillingness to try new and different approaches, an inability to learn lessons from mistakes, a tendency to blame others and ultimately failure. What are you doing to create an environment in which it is safe to fail?

Fear of rejection

Most of us will have faced rejection in our childhood and teenage years. Sometimes this can be through difficult life events such as adoption, fostering, being sent to boarding school, parents moving away and leaving a teenager in a different country (e.g. missionaries, internationally mobile workers, army personnel). Other times it can be subtler, but no less impactful, with favouritism among siblings, being left out of a peer group, not feeling that you fit in your family, or rejection due to gender and sexuality.

Whatever the cause, the impact on you as a leader is that, without being dealt with, the rejection can result in a fear of being further rejected in the workplace. This can lead to anger when your voice is not heard, to not letting people get close to you (for fear of further rejection), to not being willing to be transparent and open or to a lack of vulnerability in relationships. This is, of course, not unique to a particular generation. I have seen these behaviours in very senior members of staff in multiple organizations, but millennial leaders have a unique power as leaders of their own generation to better embrace this self-intelligence.

The impact of fear of rejection can be that team members can feel left out or emotionally disconnected. Leaders can appear aloof, remote, defensive or controlling.

The determination of someone who has experienced significant rejection to ensure that 'rejection never happens to me again' has to be experienced to be fully believed.

Are you fearful of being rejected in your own leadership?

Fear of being found out: imposter syndrome
Rachel: Millennials definitely experience imposter syndrome: the fear of being found out. It seems to be a massive issue for us. I think this is particularly because we are so aware of the world around us and so used to comparing ourselves with others in a way that older generations couldn't.

Personally, I find it's a constant struggle to not feel that you're blagging your way through life and my millennial friends tell me they feel exactly the same! I'm so thankful for all the amazing opportunities I've been given at a young age and the responsibility that I've been privileged to have, but there is a real tension I have to deal with when imposter syndrome kicks in. Even as I write this book, it seems quite unbelievable to me that I am writing a first book, only one year out of university, and the questions of whether I really should be swirl in my mind.

Similarly, having been given the honour of working with, and leading employability sessions for, survivors of human trafficking with a charity I intern for, I find myself needing to be really intentional about knowing my identity to stop the imposter syndrome saying, 'You shouldn't do this. You're too young, you're not skilled!'

Despite external evidence of their competence, those exhibiting imposter syndrome remain convinced that they are frauds and do not deserve the success they have achieved.

Proof of success is dismissed as luck, timing or as a result of deceiving others into thinking they are more intelligent and competent than they really are.

Simon: It doesn't seem to get any better the higher you go, the larger your office and the bigger your title. The feelings seem to get stronger not weaker.

The dangers associated with this fear are that you begin to hide your inadequacies, to cover up for your failures and to be devious in the way that you present information or massage it to make yourself look better than you are.

Fear of losing power

One of the most catastrophic things that can happen to an employee is to lose their job, to be forced out of an organization due to redundancy, because they are no longer needed or their skills no longer fit.

The impact on the individual can be huge, resonating through life for many years and the damage done is sometimes never restored. This impact at a human and emotional level of rejection, humiliation, fear and abandonment can often tap into unrealized fears from childhood and adolescence, and it therefore affects some people to a greater extent than others. Walking back into a leadership position following such an incident, without having had counselling or therapy, can be a daunting experience and is not for the faint-hearted.

My observations of people who have done this are that they tend to create environments of control around them. Resolved not to let the same situation happen again, they determine that whatever got out of control last time will not do so this time. It's a self-preservation mechanism, inbuilt from the beginning of time. Therefore, the tendency is to be defensive, to be careful about who is trusted with information, slow to take responsibility for mistakes and manipulative. These issues can be addressed, but need to be managed within a fully supportive, trusting and accountable environment.

For millennial leaders, it may be in this arena that they see conflict arise. Do you ever feel hungry for responsibility that is not afforded to you? Do you ever feel a coldness from people who are more senior than you are? It is important to remember *why* someone may be acting in this way towards you to enable you to navigate these relationships more empathetically and efficiently. It is also important to learn from this behaviour in others. Is your own leadership one of openness to those you are leading? Guardedness is a red flag for someone seeking to lead. It will be identified quickly as a lack of authenticity and integrity and needs to be dealt with urgently.

Table 5.1 provides a summary of the core fears experienced by millennial leaders.

Table 5.1 The five core fears

Fear	Behaviours	Results
Not being liked	Erratic, inconsistent, avoidance of hard decisions	Lack of respect for you, not being liked
Failure	Not trying, not learning lessons, not taking risks, blaming others	Failure
Rejection	Not letting people get close, lack of vulnerability, lack of transparency	Rejection
Being found out	Hiding, devious, lack of transparency	Being found out
Losing power	Blaming others, positioning, politics, manipulation	Diminished power

In the same way that our fear can lead to the very result we fear (fear of not being liked leading to not being liked, fear of failure leading to failure), the cure for the fears that hold us back from being vulnerable is equally circular: being vulnerable. We need better tools for helping us press into this vulnerability, which is just a long word that means saying out loud: please help me.

LEARNING TO BE VULNERABLE

Rachel: As leaders, we need to learn how to be appropriately vulnerable in the workplace and therefore break the shame/fear/control cycle.

Brené Brown, a psychologist who has spent her life researching shame and vulnerability, says there are three rules about shame:

1. We all have shame. It's universal and pervasive.
2. We're all afraid to talk about it.
3. The less you talk about it, the more you have it.

What are you most ashamed of? Maybe it's your family, your education, your addiction to pornography or the state of your relationships? Maybe it's your body size, your job or lack of a job? There is no doubt that social media and advertising have contributed to our culture of making us believe that ordinary is never enough. In fact that *we* can never be enough.

Never good enough, perfect enough, thin enough, powerful enough, successful enough, smart enough, certain enough, extraordinary enough. We can never have enough likes, shares, subscribers, views or reviews. And comparison magnifies our shame.

At the time when Simon was growing up, it was perhaps good enough to be the best violinist in the village, the best cricketer at school, the best artist in town, the best florist in the market. For every village, every street, every town and every city there could be a best. For our generation today, it can feel as if, unless you are the best speaker globally, the best leader nationally, the best marketer in the universe, then the good that you are is never enough.

Simon: Brené Brown discovered some really good news in her research, good news that every leader needs to hear.

First, shame loses all its power when it is named and spoken out. It withers when it is named. Its power is broken when you talk about it with someone else. This is extraordinarily good news. It puts the power to break shame within our grasp. We just have to name it.

Second, in order for shame to be broken it requires us to make ourselves vulnerable. This is not such good news. It sounds frightening. But have you noticed that we are drawn to other people's vulnerability yet repelled by our own? Why is it that when someone stands up in front of a crowd and speaks compellingly of their struggle with addiction, of the loss of a child or a loved one, of a wrestle with sexuality or gender that we lean in close, entranced with the emotions and feelings, moved by the courage and daring that it takes to expose yourself in this way? There is a deep connection. A shared humanity. A resonance with the flawed and broken human condition. A willingness to countenance that being real and authentic is a prize to be won, a trophy worth displaying.

Third, vulnerability is not weakness, it is courage and great daring. It is the willingness to let yourself be seen. It requires all your inner strength and capacity, a bold stepping-out into the wilderness, not quite knowing how you will be received.

Fourth, Brown says that 'Vulnerability is the birthplace of love, belonging, joy, courage, empathy, and creativity. It is the source of hope, empathy, accountability, and authenticity'.[5] Most of us actually believe and act as if the reverse is true; as if vulnerability is the birthplace of disconnection, hopelessness and despair. Therefore, it takes courage to step out and put this into practice.

OUT OF YOUR COMFORT ZONE

Rachel: As we have seen, my generation is at an advantage in that we already understand the importance of this to a point but, as many of us already know, it's vital that we let our identities shape and grow. Identity is a life-long journey.

As I've mentioned, a sense of purpose in my life around injustice has been significant for me from a young age. Towards the end of sixth form, a sense of greater purpose was on my mind and I decided to defer my university place for a year and take a gap year. I wanted something that would help me to understand my identity, to practically help others and to go on an adventure outside my comfort zone. So, I moved to Canada for five months on a leadership course that was definitely out of my comfort zone.

Running each morning in weather that reached minus 25 degrees and living in a wooden hut next to a frozen lake while working alongside a community struggling with gang crime and addiction was all very uncomfortable! It was an adventure. It was a journey. And it helped me to grasp more of who I was. I was stripped of all that I knew, friends, family and culture, and it gave me the opportunity to really look at myself. Who was I when nobody else was around? What was my identity without my family and my friends? It was 'tiny' me discovering more of who I was in a very big Canada and I loved it.

This pushing out of my comfort zone saw my identity shaped in a new way. The same can be learnt through the trial and error of leaders before us. Bev Kauffeldt, part of the team at Samaritan's Purse, thought she knew her identity pretty well before she found herself working on the ground in Monrovia, Liberia, during the Ebola epidemic of 2014. The daily ordeal of seeing people fighting against death and often losing, knowing that her own life was on the line and at risk, was almost too much. Bev is an amazing leader who headed up the team ensuring that the dead bodies were disposed of well and safely and that the doctors and nurses followed correct procedure. As a result, she had the potential every moment of every day to be exposed to the bodily fluids that could so easily kill her.

Sharing her experiences with Forge Leadership, Bev tells the remarkable story of how this impacted her identity at a deep, core level:

> I learned a very, very tough lesson during Ebola where I thought I knew where my identity was. But when everything all of a sudden is taken from you and you don't know if you'll ever get it back, that's something that you never forget. And if you don't learn from that then you're a fool. So, when I'm making decisions it's not an ego thing. It's not trying to prove myself. It's not putting false expectations on my staff. It's letting them first and foremost know what their identity is. And when you understand that and are able to grasp that again, and it's a daily struggle sometimes, there's an absolute freedom in serving because it's not about you and, if everything was taken away, it doesn't matter. Because your identity can never be taken away.

> I think that, unfortunately, and I regret it, it took me my first 15 years of being overseas to really get it and an incredible crisis, probably the worst crisis of my life, to really have that right smack in front of my face. To really answer the question, 'Where is your identity?' And so I think, for me, that has

completely shifted my thought process every day with every interaction.[6]

Leaders everywhere can learn from Bev's experience. How can we take the time now to know ourselves, our true selves, better so that when crisis strikes we can lead out of who we are? And how can we process our leadership experiences, the good, the bad and the ugly, to become even more secure in our identity, dealing with our fears and learning to lead out of this place of vulnerability?

Chapter six

INTEGRITY – WHY GOODNESS CAN BE MORE VALUABLE THAN GREATNESS

> **Mark 2:** Millennial leaders have a strong moral compass, are able to articulate their core values and beliefs and have developed the discipline of aligning their decisions and actions with those beliefs.

WHY INTEGRITY IS SO VITAL FOR LEADERS OF THE FUTURE

Gen Y (Millennials) will force businesses to align words and action.[1]

Rachel: In our research, millennials were asked, 'Which of these characteristics have you observed in the most effective leaders? Please choose the three most relevant.' (See Figure 6.1 overleaf.)

Integrity was high with over 55 per cent of people listing it in their top three. It was followed closely only by humility, but more on that later.

However, interviewees also often quoted integrity as being a significant challenge: 'It's a challenge to . . . stand up for what is right rather than back "whoever shouts the loudest".'

On the flip side, integrity was also listed as one of the unique contributions millennials feel they will bring to leadership.

Simon: So, what do we mean by 'integrity'?

Which of these characteristics have you observed in the most effective leaders? Please select the 3 most relevant.

442 respondents

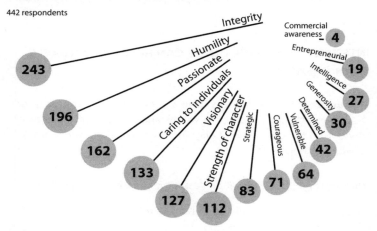

Figure 6.1 Characteristics of the most effective leaders

The *Oxford English Dictionary* has two definitions: 'The quality of being honest and having strong moral principles' and 'The state of being whole and undivided'.

Definition 1: the quality of being honest and having strong moral principles

To act with integrity, you must first know who you are. That's why integrity always follows identity.

You must know what you stand for, what you believe in and what you care most about. You can't be honest or true to something that is constantly shifting or is relative.

In a millennial business world where there is great uncertainty, millennials are respecting leaders who know their core values and beliefs.

This is truly remarkable in a Western society that is told to be accepting of every view and opinion and that, if it's true for you that's fine, but it's only true for you.

But maybe it's not quite so remarkable.

Rachel: Maybe, just maybe, millennials are looking to follow windsurfers who are already riding the waves.

Maybe we're looking for stable reference points; for people who are willing to be true to themselves, to stand out from the crowd and to be real about what they believe and who they truly and fully are.

No doubt social media, global access, undercover journalism and the drive for transparency have played a huge part in ensuring that the challenge to live with integrity is greater than it ever has been. Purely because there is a bigger chance of your duplicity being found out!

The recent #MeToo campaign has also highlighted the willingness and ability of those who have been abused to stand up and have their voices heard and to expose abuses of power and trust.

This is about personal credibility.

Simon: And in order to have credibility, you must first be able to clearly *articulate* your deeply held beliefs. After all, you are only ever as convincing as you are convinced or, to put it another way, the message is only as believable as the messenger. The research told us that millennials can spot inconsistency between word and deed from a mile away: 'I think the worst leaders [are] probably inconsistent in their character . . . the ones where you're unsure about how they will respond in a situation because they don't have that integrity of character.'

And when, as you will as a leader, you are making hundreds of decisions a day on what you do and what you say, without a core set of underlying principles to guide you, those decisions will lead you to surf in every random direction. The wind will blow you where it will.

As a millennial leader, your essential beliefs

1   inform your decisions;
2   enable you to say no;
3   enable your self-evaluation.

As Kouzes and Posner put it in their bestselling leadership book, *The Leadership Challenge*:

> We all know deep down that people can only speak the truth when speaking in their own true voice . . . If the words that you speak are not your words but someone else's you will not, in the long term be able to be consistent in word and deed.[2]

Kouzes and Posner continue:

> To find your voice you have to explore the inner territory. You have to take a journey into those places in your heart and soul where you bury your treasures, so that you can carefully examine them and eventually bring them out for display.[3]

Anything else is play-acting. Or fake imitation. Or fraud. Or deception.

More than ever, the millennial leadership journey demands a tough and rigorous examination of the inner self: an in-depth medical that we usually only reserve for our physical bodies. And it requires the courage to turn over a few stones (maybe lots of stones) to find out what's underneath.

Sometimes that's ugly.

It requires bravery to ask the difficult questions around motivation, such as 'Why do you really want to be a leader? Is it to prove a point? To your parents? To show someone that they were wrong? Is it to find acceptance and belonging? That sense of finding out who you are through what you do? What's driving you?'

You see, there is a dark side to leadership.

If we are to succeed as millennial leaders, we need to understand that dark side, come to terms with it and deal with it, or it will return to eat us. And it will devour those around us in the process.

Transactional analysis identifies five key positive values (see Table 6.1 overleaf) that have extremely positive drivers, perhaps drivers that made you want to be a leader in the first place. However, at their extreme they can result in negative values and negative impacts on the workplace and those around us.[4]

Rachel: From the research, 'be perfect' and 'please others' seem to be particular dangers for millennials, with our self-confessions that being afraid to make mistakes and wanting the approval of others were major risks that we were concerned would affect our leadership.

Table 6.1 Positive values and their results

Positive values	Result in messages	Result in drivers	Negative values
Achievement, autonomy, success, being right	Don't: make a mistake, take risks, be natural, be childlike	Be perfect	Extremely driven, overly demanding, pedantic
Consideration, kindness, service	Don't: be assertive, be different, be important, say no	Please others	Inconsistent, workaholic
Courage, strength, reliability	Don't: show your feelings, give in, ask for help	Be strong	Loner, lack of vulnerability, isolated
Persistence, patience, determination	Don't: be satisfied, relax, give up	Try hard	Workaholic, stressed
Speed, efficiency, responsiveness	Don't: take too long, relax, waste time	Hurry up	Overly focused, demanding

Definition 2: The state of being whole and undivided

Simon: We all know the feeling. I had just spoken to an audience of over a thousand government officials about the importance of getting all government services online. It was around 1999/2000 and the concept of online tax returns, online driving licence applications, online prescriptions and medical appointments was only a figment of most people's imaginations, dreams or nightmares.

I was young and out to make an impression and, to make a point, I slightly over-egged the pudding in my description of myself and what I had already achieved in my career. It sounded wonderful and very impressive, but wasn't exactly what you would call the whole truth.

Afterwards, as I made my way home on the train, I started to shake and sweat. In the middle of the following night, my inner critic caused mayhem and started replaying the words over and over and over again. How could I have been so stupid and naïve? The imagined consequences began to rise up repeatedly in my mind. I was mortified and vowed to never allow that to happen again.

The following morning, I tried to explain myself to my boss and to be honest. He wasn't the least bit interested. It was a minor issue to him and certainly not one that warranted sleepless nights.

My onstage self was not aligned with my backstage self. I had been inconsistent with who I knew I was. I had allowed the drivers of acceptance and affirmation to lead me down a path of wanting to be loved and accepted and had created a situation that ultimately left me feeling trapped and confused.

Rachel: This is what it feels like for millennial leaders, people wired to hold integrity so close to the core, when our inner selves don't line up with who we portray ourselves to be. And it's exhausting and stress-inducing and troublesome. It's what happens when we don't bring the whole of ourselves to the table and when we don't align what people see with who we are.

How then can we tackle the inconsistencies that arise in leadership? How can we truly be whole and full of integrity? Let's explore some ideas.

HOW NOT TO BE A FRAUD

Simon: There is, I'm afraid, no getting away from a deep internal journey that takes time, energy and effort. It's a journey that won't be easy and will involve tears, truth-telling, journaling, exploration and questioning.

It will, no doubt, involve others, be they professionals such as counsellors, therapists and pastors, or friends who are prepared to walk the rocky path, with its detours and diversions.

For me, so far it has involved counselling and therapy, and monthly sessions with my pastor. I know I'm not unique in that and, honestly, there should be a fund for every millennial leader to ensure that they take this seriously and invest in their own mental, physical and spiritual well-being.

The unique circumstances of all our childhoods and teenage years, the years when we can so easily be moulded and shaped, left for me an overwhelming feeling that I could never be good enough. I could never please anyone enough. I could never be enough.

I needed to go deeply back into my past, identifying moments at school when I had felt hurt and rejected. This meant going back and identifying the moments that still, today, resonate loudly and clearly at a decibel level much greater than the original incident.

Journeys like these are crucial in finding and dealing with the wounds and hurts that have had an impact on us.

For some, I know this has meant dealing with grief and loss, trauma and anger, due to their voices not being heard.

What is it that is causing you to be angry or to overreact today?

Rachel: There are no shortcuts to integrity. We have to put in the effort and be intentional. My experience so far on the journey to wholeness has included, like Simon, talking through deep issues, journaling and reflecting. I know I have a long way to go, but I really see that this is a journey worth taking.

IDENTIFYING YOUR CORE VALUES

Simon: Hopefully, by now you're convinced that finding you inner voice is a necessary and important part of becoming a millennial leader who is full of integrity, and you're ready to start work.

There are a number of exercises that are frequently used to enable you to identify your core values. All these exercises have been well tested by psychologists and leadership development practitioners.

Take some time to really develop your core values and dialogue them with friends. Keep your core values to a small number, five maximum, and utilize them to help you start making decisions that come from your core inner convictions.

My five core values from my reflections are

1   to seek the well-being of others;
2   to develop younger leaders;
3   to create an environment of excellence and grace;
4   to care for myself;
5   to pursue contentment through making a difference in my
     career.

These values define more *how* I do things than *what* I do, and therefore they define more of me than the activities I'm involved in.

KNOW WHAT YOU BELIEVE IN THE WORKPLACE

Simon: Just as important as articulating your core values is articulating the core beliefs underlying these values. What do you believe? Really? I don't mean in a religious sense. I mean what do you believe about yourself, your organization, your work, your leadership, the people around you and what motivates them? And what do you believe about change and technology and the environment in which you operate?

Rachel and I have some core beliefs in all these areas. In other areas, our beliefs are still being formed. I recently spent some time reflecting by the coast, writing down the core beliefs I hold dear. These beliefs inform my decisions and my actions consistently in any given situation, working as predictors for how I will act. They are a proxy for who I am, but they are not all of who I am.

In completing this exercise, I sought to answer some specific questions, which may be helpful for you too. As I tried to articulate my core beliefs, I asked myself a number of things:

1 What do you believe about yourself?
2 What do you believe about your organization?
3 What do you believe about work?
4 What do you believe about leadership?
5 What do you believe about people?
6 What do you believe about motivation?
7 What do you believe about change?

In answering these questions and comparing the answers with each other's, Rachel and I further understood our overlapping and diverging approaches to work. For example, when responding to the question, 'What do you believe about yourself?' I answered:

I believe that I have a specific set of leadership gifts that are best suited to leading large organizations through periods of transition. I believe I have intrinsic value through who I am. I believe that my value is not determined by what I achieve.

Whereas Rachel answered:

I believe that my value is not determined by what I do, but who I am. I believe I am a better version of myself when I am living in community.

Grasping your beliefs is not only helpful in dialogue with others but in better knowing and understanding yourself.

What are your core beliefs as a millennial leader?

WHEN YOUR INTEGRITY IS CHALLENGED

Simon: Once you have articulated your core values and beliefs, there will come moments in your leadership career when they are sorely and deeply tried. Moments when they are pushed to the extremities. Moments that Professor Bobby Clinton categorizes as crisis, conflict, life crisis, leadership backlash or isolation.[5]

These are moments of severe stress that at one time or another will have an impact on the life of a leader. They are often associated with the deepening and expansion of a leader's influence when handled in accordance with a set of understood core values and beliefs.

Rachel: It's important, as many of us enter the key years of our millennial leadership journey, that we understand that these events are quite normal and happen at regular intervals for everyone. The wisdom from older leaders is that we must learn to recognize these events in our lives so that we know best how to respond.

For millennial leaders who hold integrity in such high regard, the potential to be broken and to feel extreme pressure in such circumstances is likely to be heightened. Therefore, the need for a clarity of core values and beliefs and to have processes that align actions with words is even more critical.

Our ability to process these events, learn from them and grow through them is vital. Each one has the potential to take a millennial leader out, but each one also has the ability to form a deeper sense of integrity and identity in the life of a millennial leader.

Simon: That has certainly been true for me. We had been working for several years on the rebranding of the UK arm of an organization I was involved in. It had been a long process, involving consultants, the senior leadership team and most of the staff. Away days, workshops, focus groups, questionnaires and much heartsearching had formed the final result, which we were all proud of and very excited about. Websites were being designed, logos finalized and brochures printed.

During the whole of that time, I had kept my global colleagues informed, travelled to present to them and keep them in the picture and had dialogued with my board of directors. As with most significant change, nodding assent had been given and even encouragement and support.

And then I started to hear murmurings; sounds that indicated a degree of discomfort from among some board members with the direction of travel. When it came to the crunch, the board listened and decided against implementation. They were very clear. We had done nothing wrong, the process had been engaging and engaged. However, some of those involved in the decision making had not realized the impact of the decision.

This was leadership backlash in a very focused way.

Looking back, I can see how this was the right decision and a bold and brave one. At the time, I was gutted. How could I carry on? How could I walk back in the following morning and explain to staff and senior team what had happened? How would they react? What would they think of me?

What I learned through that process was that it was as much how I responded to the leadership backlash as the leadership backlash itself that defined me.

The ability to be humble, admit mistakes, face up to failure, pick myself up again and face difficult decisions and conversations with grace, strength and the ability to say to people, 'If we're going to get through this, then I need your help' ultimately made me a better leader; a more integral leader; a leader whom others would follow even when the going got tough.

This was a true integrity check, one in which my values of creating an environment of excellence and grace, pursuing the well-being of others and caring for myself while pushing through to make a difference, were sorely tested.

I remained in the role of leader of that organization for another seven years following that event, years in which the organization grew substantially and in which I and others would say my leadership flourished.

ALIGNING YOUR DECISIONS WITH YOUR VALUES AND BELIEFS

Rachel: For millennial leaders, aligning decisions to our values and beliefs requires work and effort and is extremely important to us.

Yet our natural reaction is to align our decisions with our own experience or with what the data is telling us or with the immediate needs around us.

How can we change that?

Align personal values and beliefs with organizational values and beliefs

We were told by 89 per cent of millennial leaders that it is extremely important or important that the ethos and values of the workplace matched their own values (see Figure 6.2).

How important is it that the ethos and values of your workplace match your own values?
442 respondents

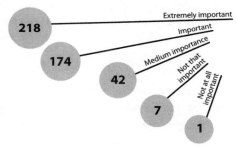

Figure 6.2 Workplace and personal ethos and values

Simon: This is critical to moving forward.

Once you have articulated your own values and beliefs, it is vitally important to examine them against those of the organization you work for. Is there a clash? Do you detect areas of conflict and discomfort?

In one organization I led, we had always had a two-page list of organizational values that no one could remember. Every year at appraisal time, everyone would be asked how they were doing against the set of values that we held as an organization. This was good progress, but it was pretty meaningless the rest of the year because no one could remember what these values were the day after their appraisal!

As I examined my own personal values, in 2007 we went through a process of clarifying and distilling our values down into this simple statement: 'We are committed to the highest levels of excellence delivered with abounding grace.'

This became a phrase I would use to explain the values of the organization to every new employee. It became a phrase we would keep coming back to at our team meetings and executive meetings. It was a phrase packed with meaning and one that we could hold one another accountable to.

It is clear from the research that, for millennials, aligning their own personal values with those of the organization they lead is an important step in being able to lead with integrity.

Report back on values

More and more organizations are making sure that, as part of their corporate reporting, they report back on how things are done, on their behaviours and how these have matched their values.

This is not so much about what they have achieved but about how they have achieved it.

It can include admitting mistakes, things that have gone wrong, areas that are currently being investigated, standards that have been met or missed, commitments to transparency, ethics or the environment, commitments to customers, complaints procedures, customer return policies or simply how staff have been rewarded and thanked.

James Clear goes a step further with his own personal yearly 'Integrity Report'. In his 2016 report,[6] he asks three simple yet critical questions that we would all do well to review on a yearly basis, if not more regularly.

1   What are the core values that drive my life and work?
2   How am I living and working with integrity right now?
3   How can I set a higher standard in the future?

In his response to these questions, Clear identifies areas where he has made improvements over the past year, including admitting his mistakes and areas where he can further improve, for example by being more consistent and more thankful.

Clear's example is a great one that encourages a rhythm of transparency, humility and vulnerability. It's a millennial leader's response to a changing business environment.

THE IMPORTANCE OF LONG-TERM ACCOUNTABILITY AND MENTORING IN ENSURING INTEGRITY

Rachel: There are some really encouraging trends in the research and in the literature, which suggest that we are much more open to constant feedback, accountability and development on a personal, one-to-one basis than our predecessors. In fact, it's more than being more open. We really desire it.

We have already seen that, in part, this can be attributed to a culture of instant feedback through gaming and social media.[7]

We tend to approach work as a constant learning experience and therefore long to receive immediate feedback, with our strengths and successes being acknowledged.[8]

In our research interviews, millennials were very proactive in seeking mentors and 87 per cent reported having had a mentor.

As one leader commented:

> I think once you have been benefited yourself from being well mentored you understand its value. As a leader, I need to make sure I carve that out for others. I think there's no shortcut to having time with people because it gives you time to talk and be a role model.

Worryingly though, the research also showed that our experience of the mentoring received is mixed, with over 40 per cent rating the experience as ineffective or of medium effectiveness (see Figure 6.3).

If you have had a mentor, how would you rate the effectiveness of the mentoring you received?
385 respondents

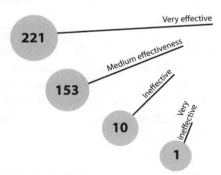

Figure 6.3 Effectiveness of mentoring

Simon: If the level of integrity is to increase in millennial leaders then the effectiveness of mentoring also needs to increase.

Intentionality and consistency are vitally important in a mentoring relationship. Without these, then issues of long-term commitment to values and beliefs, the processing of integrity checks and the ability to become vulnerable in the context of a long-term relationship are difficult to achieve.

I personally have benefited from a long-term mentor to whom I can be accountable. Over a 20-year journey with Simon Harris, who happens to be my church pastor, we have gone through life crises, isolation, despair, hope, joy, challenge, support and celebration. Nothing is off-limits. We have had periods where we have met less often, times when our relationship has been strained, times when we have met weekly and times when we don't sit down for a couple of months.

The constant routine over all those years is to put monthly lunches or coffees in the diary every December for the following year. I honestly don't know how I would have survived as a leader without Simon's continual companionship for the journey and his willingness to stick by me through the thick and the thin of it all.

Despite what all the management books will tell you, there is no recipe or formula to make this happen. There is no list of questions that we always use, or set of techniques to go through. It is just raw, human communication, with the tears, whoops of joy and bewilderment that characterize any long-term mentoring or accountability relationship.

Leading the millennial way involves pursuing a mentor.

Be prepared to commit to long-term journeying, wherever that may take you. You may not see the benefit for years to come, but you will look back in your forties and fifties and give thanks and rejoice at the richness that such a relationship has brought into your life.

Here are my top tips on what to look for in an ideal integrity mentor:

- high support and high challenge
- totally trustworthy
- outside your current situation
- empathetic
- high on emotional intelligence
- humble
- a listener
- straight talking
- willing to wrestle with issues rather than give answers
- values based
- committed for the long term
- mutual benefit.

Chapter seven

INNER STRENGTH

The future doesn't belong to the brilliant but the resilient. Not to those who avoid scars or pain but to wounded healers who choose to give again.

Alan Scott[1]

Mark 3: Millennial leaders have developed an inner strength through establishing rhythms of life that enable them to persevere and bounce back, whatever is thrown at them.

Rachel: As mentioned earlier, when I was 17, I climbed Mount Kilimanjaro. At 5,895 metres, this was rather daunting! I took physical preparation seriously, running and training in the gym, which also built mental resilience when running up that hill 'just one more time'.

Yet this was nothing compared to the mental strength I had to draw on for summit day.

Waking up after a couple of hours' sleep at midnight to snow and altitude sickness, I prepped my kit for the day, put on my head torch and we set off. I was already exhausted, cold and sick and I had a 16-hour climb ahead of me.

Physically, I wanted to turn back, but I knew I had trained for this moment. The daily preparation was all leading up to this and the resilience that had increased in the previous few months was what I now needed to draw on.

I made it to the summit and it was so worth it!

The view was breathtaking and I knew that my inner strength was being developed for all the challenges that lay ahead.

WHY INNER STRENGTH IS CRITICAL TO MILLENNIAL LEADERS

Simon: There is one thing for certain as a leader. You are going to get knocked down. There'll be moments when all the stuffing will be knocked out of you and you'll be left breathless, head spinning and dazed. Millennial leadership is not for the faint-hearted. We've already seen how demanding the environment in which millennials are leading is.

In our research, millennial leaders reported understanding the need to build resilience into their lives by developing rhythms that work. Of course, resilience encompasses so much more than balance and rhythms in life, but when speaking with millennial leaders, resilience and whole-life balance were very much linked in their minds.

Rachel: Millennial leaders said that trying to get a 'really good balance in life' was vital, understanding that exercise affects sleep, which affects productivity. Work–life balance was closely linked to this idea of whole-life balance and creating resilience, with millennial leaders explaining they put aside rest days and control their own diaries to ensure space and balance: 'I control my diary, so I work really hard at saying no.'

Others described planning rhythms within their lives to create a sense of whole-life balance, explaining, 'I always take a rest day. Two days off a week. Always a retreat day every month: that's in the diary for the whole year before everything else is.'

Another interviewee gave further insight into whole-life balance. He reported asking himself reflective questions such as: How much time have I spent with my wife this past week? How much sleep have I got? Have I been committed to my hockey team? Do I feel like I've been able to be at church . . . honouring commitments there?'

The theory is there, as millennial leaders describe behaviours and rhythms in their lives to build balance and resilience, yet they expressed a struggle with implementing these in practice.

Learning from experience, one millennial leader explained the need to draw healthy boundaries to achieve a satisfying whole-life balance:

> Sometimes you just need to stop. There's always more you can do, and learning what you can do and when you should say no can be challenging. And how do you draw the boundaries when you've got to lead loads of other people?

Millennials are taking up positions of leadership in an always-on world. It is a journey, but one that they are tackling with a growing understanding of the importance of resilience and balance. One millennial leader, for example, speaks of her journey like this:

> I started out as an intern . . . I set really good boundaries for my first couple of years and then when I took on my first leadership role where I was responsible for a whole team and I was very accountable . . . I definitely . . . worked way too long. To the point where it got quite bad and I had to say to my manager: 'My stress level, it's really really impacting my life outside work and it's not acceptable.'
>
> So since then I've been quite ruthless really about my time. I'm involved at work in our well-being group where we try

and tackle some of these issues around work-life balance, resilience and saying no . . . So I am quite ruthless and when I started my most recent job I said to my manager, 'I'm really ruthless about my work. I will go to the gym at lunch some-times, this is the time I get in, I work from home one day a week. I will always leave by 5.30.' . . . I've set myself really strong boundaries and I think that's really important as well when you're a leader, for other people to see you setting the boundaries.

With increasing awareness of mental health issues among us,[2] the signs from the research are that millennial leaders are taking the issue of wholeness and well-being extremely seriously, and that this is having an impact on the way they think and act at work, and the cultures they are seeking to create.

HOW CAN WE INCREASE OUR RESILIENCE?

Simon: Windsurfers train specifically to increase their resilience and their core inner strength. During long tacks, windsurfers maintain body tension to continually convert the wind power from the sail into forwards motion through the board. Less body tension means more energy is lost and they are not able to take full advantage of the sail. For windsurfers, this is the equivalent of running a marathon.

I think this is an area where millennial leaders can learn from the mistakes and successes of those who have gone before them, particularly those who have finished well.

I remember the first question I ever asked a main board director of a FTSE 100 company. I was a young graduate, a few years out of university, and I'd been invited to an event for 'high potentials'. The director, who was in his forties, talked at length about the value of personal development, the openness of the company to enabling people to take risks and the opportunity to succeed.

My mind was buzzing with a question as I really wanted to know how to be as successful as he was. So, with my heart in my mouth, I stuttered, 'What has made you so successful?'

I'll never forget his answer: 'Well, I get knocked down more times than everyone else. I've just learnt to get up a lot quicker. When everyone else around you is falling down, pick yourself up, dust yourself down and continue making a difference.'

At the time, I couldn't really comprehend what this senior leader meant. Why did this make him a good leader? Over the years, though, I have come to appreciate resilience as a key character trait in the leaders around me.

What I've noticed in the great leaders I've observed closely is that they have a unique ability to keep a positive attitude and to lead with purpose despite the circumstances, and to not take being knocked down personally.

Rachel: Millennial leaders are human. We have emotions, feelings, concerns, worries and thoughts like those we are leading but, if we are to succeed in the long term, we have to train differently for crisis moments; we have to prepare differently. We have to focus on our own resilience and inner strength and take critical steps to address the weaknesses in our own armour.

LEARNING TO GET UP QUICKLY

Simon: So how can you develop inner strength as a leader? Indeed, can you develop it, or is it something you're born with?

Debbie Duncan in her book, *The Art of Daily Resilience*, describes resilience like this:

> Resilience is a term we use to express how we can bounce back from an awful event or personal tragedy. It is about having the personal strength to complete the course, to reach the end of the road. It is not a concrete asset, something we learn once and then we use again. Our resilience may vary over time.[3]

Debbie goes on to talk about the need to look at resilience holistically: 'We are aware that body, mind, and spirit interact. To strengthen our overall resilience, we need to learn how to improve resilience in each of these areas.'

In other words, developing resilience is hard, daily work. It is the storing up of resources and capacity so that we are able to be ready to respond when the moment comes.

For 14 years, I led an emergency response charity. Our reputation was based on the fact that we could be the first to get to the scene of a humanitarian disaster with skilled people, money, resources and capacity.

I remember sitting in the restaurant of P. F. Changs in Charlotte, North Carolina, as news broke of the catastrophic magnitude 7.0 earthquake hitting Haiti on Tuesday 12 January 2010.

An estimated three million people were affected by the quake and, although we didn't know it then, over 200,000 people were to die.

I was surrounded by the global leadership of the disaster relief organization I was working for. As the news reports began to hit CNN, phones were already ringing, and small groups started to form around our Chinese meal as plans to deploy planes, helicopters, people, tarpaulins, water filter units and medical supplies were formed within moments.

Water was a critical need and we planned to get five water filtration units to Haiti within 24 hours.

That was only possible because of the years of preparation that had gone into this moment: pre-positioning of supplies into a forward base at Florida; preparation of people through trainings, real-life simulations, drills and personal study; the purchasing of supplies, warehouses, transport hubs and routes had all prepared us to be able to deploy this quickly. And the access to private funding that had already been fundraised for meant that we could act without waiting for government grants or approvals.

Millennial leaders know that hurricanes and earthquakes are going to happen. Maybe they will be even more frequent in the future. Therefore they know the importance of preparation.

SOURCES OF INNER STRENGTH

Simon: During my time studying at Fuller Seminary, through their Master of Arts in Global Leadership, I came to appreciate the strength that monastic traditions have to bring to forming daily disciplines that can build inner strength and fortitude. As I studied the Benedictine rule of life, and indeed developed my own rule of life, I became aware of the incredible way in which these rules of life build resilience into body, mind and spirit holistically.

But can these rules be applied to those who have no faith at all?

In an article in the *Financial Times* called 'Work, Rest and Pray', the authors comment: 'We suspected that there might be aspects of monastic life that those who share this yearning can learn from, without having to take on board its religious commitments and beliefs.'[4]

Even if something essential is lost when faith is removed, non-believers still have plenty to gain.

As the responsibilities of leadership have grown, getting the rhythm of life right has become more and more important to me. If I'm too busy, I'm of little or no use to anyone.

HOW'S YOUR RHYTHM OF LIFE?

Simon: Over the years, I've managed to miss that all-important single clash of the cymbals at the end of an orchestral piece and have played a song in the wrong time signature at someone's wedding! I also can't dance in time, have two left feet and always come in singing at the wrong moment. For a music graduate, that's all rather embarrassing. Maybe it explains why it's taken me over 40 years to really get a grip on getting the rhythm of my life to work for me and those I love.

That's why I'm passionate as I work with millennial leaders about helping them get their rhythms of life right and appropriate for each stage of life.

Call it work–life balance or getting the balance right or preventing stress and burnout, our research showed that millennial leaders struggle with it. So, here's what I've learnt along the way:

1 If there is not space to be still, everything else suffers: **be still**.
2 If there is not space to keep fit and healthy through exercise, sleep and rest, everything else suffers: **care for yourself**.

3 If there is not space to 'fill your tank' with things that you enjoy spending time doing, everything else suffers: **fill your tank**.

4 If there is not space to spend quality time with those really close to you, they suffer and you do as well: **build relationships**.

5 If there is not space to build authentic community, everything else suffers: **build community**.

How is your rhythm of life? I encourage you to experiment with different practices in each of the above areas and see what works for you. For example, in order to 'be still' I now take a weekly Sabbath day of complete rest from work, I pray and read my Bible each day and retreat for a week each year. Similarly, Rachel tries to take one day of rest every week and to have a moment each day to read the Bible.

In order to make sure I am 'building relationships', I have a date with my wife every week, have friends around for dinner once a month, take on the role of mentor to one young person and take time every day to listen to someone's needs and to talk personally about non-task related issues. Rachel builds relationships by inviting people to share a meal together each week, having a date night with her husband every week and seeks to regularly meet for coffee with friends to catch up and encourage one another.

I'm learning that in implementing these rhythms, even sporadically, I see my inner strength growing. I feel stronger in body, mind and soul, enriched and with a greater sense of perspective on the significant business issues that come across my desk every day.

Rachel: For much of our generation the focus on relationships and on whole-life flourishing means that rhythm is taking on a bigger and bigger role. The growth of reflective practices has brought significant attention to working out how best to recharge, how best to pace yourself and to ensure that you are focused and fresh for work.

THE CONTRIBUTION OF PERSPECTIVE TO INNER STRENGTH

Simon: When questioned about what most helped them to bounce back from failure, millennial leaders often quoted the need to keep perspective.

For me, my weekly Friday lunchtime walks created a rhythm that allowed me to keep that perspective. My own experience led me to evolve practices that came out of that experience and included

1 finding mechanisms to enable me to get the big picture on what is happening by talking regularly to people outside the situation;
2 continually clarifying my purpose and direction and staying focused on that purpose;
3 remembering that it's not all about me and not thinking too highly of myself, or too lowly;
4 learning to laugh at myself and not to take myself too seriously;
5 processing quickly whenever I get knocked down and getting others to process with me.

If millennial leadership is all about leading people into the best future possible for them, then we need to develop resilient character as millennial leaders, character that keeps a future perspective and a future orientation and that has a good perspective of where the horizon is.

This is not arrogance, it comes from an inner strength. It's an ability (or character) to humbly acknowledge our humanness and failure, and yet also see that we were made for greater things than this.

Chapter eight

INSIGHT

Mark 4: Millennial leaders have developed a deep insight by creating space for perspective, reflection and planning and enabling themselves and their teams to connect with their emotions.

Rachel: Millennial leaders find that when boundaries are blurred, it's difficult to find space to pause and reflect. Yet in a chaotic world, the need for millennials to bring deep insight and reflection to complex problems was readily recognized by the millennials we interviewed. A massive question we have is how we as leaders can create space for the creativity we eagerly desire.

THEN THE SILENCE FELL

Simon: *Dr Who* fans like me were gripped by the motif of 'the Silence' that ran through the final series of Matt Smith's incarnation as the Doctor, when he was told, 'The Pandorica will open and silence will fall.' According to *Dr Who* fans, 'the Silence' may be a form of life that came into being before the universe existed when there was only 'the Silence': no planets, no life as we know it, nothing.

Silence, of course, can be very awkward; in a room of strangers, for example, when no one knows what to say next and you're afraid of filling the silence with nonsense (although some people don't seem to be that afraid of doing that!).

Silence can also be used to manipulate people. It can be scary or a rare commodity. But silence can also be awesome, such as when you're caught up in the wonder of nature, standing in awe of the stars or at the top of a mountain.

These are times when I have let my words be few.

Millennial leaders need to let the silence fall more often. To allow the space to think and reflect. This chapter is all about how we can be more present in the moment, get greater insight into what is really going on around us, achieve greater perspective, connect better with the world and, as a result, be better millennial leaders.

BEING PRESENT IN THE MOMENT

Simon: An experienced leader whom we can learn from in this respect is Baroness Cox. She has been a champion of human rights and has spoken in the UK Parliament for over thirty years on behalf of those who have no voice. On the Forge Leadership podcast, she said this about living in the present moment:

> There's another phrase that I find very helpful and that is the 'sacrament of the present moment'. All we ever have is the present moment. There's no point in living with regrets or nostalgia for the past. That's been . . . There's no point in worrying about the future . . . just . . . live in that present moment to the full and give it your all.[1]

Great wisdom that rang true with many millennials we interviewed.

Millennials get that this is about being in the moment. Being present. Focusing on the people and issue at hand. Really focusing.

How can we do that in practice?

One of the techniques I have used to help me in this is to create a 'for later' notebook that is always at hand.

I learned this technique from a doctor during a time of extreme stress. I was in the midst of my telecoms career and had been on secondment to another telecoms organization on the rollout of a significant national project. This involved me driving for three hours a day to get to the organization's headquarters where the team I was leading was based.

After five months of this, I was totally exhausted and, at that early point in my career, did not have the skills to cope well with the pressure and stress. It got to the point where I would spend every weekend in bed with exhaustion and then to the point where I couldn't move or walk or sleep. I ended up signed off work for six weeks with mental and physical exhaustion. The lack of sleep was the major factor affecting me and I asked the doctor what to do about this. I would get off to sleep well but then wake in the middle of the night with issues on my mind, and my mind would then go round and round for hours trying to solve the problem.

The doctor simply suggested creating a 'for the morning' notebook to put by the side of my bed and cultivating the practice of writing down the issue that was disturbing me in it, closing it and lying back down again.

And it worked. In fact, it worked miraculously. I don't have a notebook by the side of my bed any more. I don't need it. But I do keep a notebook in the office labelled 'for later'. I will journal in it ideas that come or issues that distract during the day that are not immediately relevant to the task at hand and that are 'for later'.

Another way of dealing with this in a team context is to have an item on the agenda at the beginning of a meeting, tabled for no longer than 15 minutes, entitled 'Top of Mind'. This enables anyone on the team to raise anything that is distracting them there and then that will stop them from focusing on the topics and purpose of the meeting they are in. This does two things.

First, it re-focuses people on the actual topic of the meeting. Second, it allows processing time (albeit a small amount of time) for those who have rushed into the meeting with a significant issue that they are dealing with to offload and have part of their burden lifted, increasing the possibility of their engagement in the meeting.

CREATING SPACE IN OUR ORGANIZATIONS FOR INSIGHT TO FUNCTION WELL

Rachel: We need to create space and perspective for ourselves to function well as millennial leaders. We also need to create space within our organizations for insight, deep, meaningful, thoughtful engagement, in order for them to function well too.

Millennial leaders, with their focus on relationship and community, get this intuitively. The best organizations are ones where the relationships flourish and, in order to do that, those relationships need time and space to breathe.

Simon: Our employees are not automatons. They are not robots and the rhythms of our organizations need to create the space for reflection.

Rarely have I found in my career examples of leaders who do this well, but there are a few notable outliers to learn from.

I had a wonderful first boss, Nick Forse, who tragically died of cancer at a young age while I was working for him. Nick led a group doing research into speech recognition technologies and he knew how to motivate and focus the group to produce excellent results and win awards. But he also knew how to have fun.

Every Friday afternoon, we were allowed and expected to have Friday afternoon projects. These were projects that weren't on the critical delivery list, but that used our creativity and ingenuity to push the boundaries of technology that bit further and create new breakthroughs and insights that we couldn't have achieved if we were always delivering code and hardware for the current project.

In one organization I led, we examined our organizational rhythm of life in a very focused way. What were we doing to foster a sense of community? What were we doing to put into practice our purpose and mission on a practical, local and individual level. What were we doing to create space for people to reflect and plan?

Our daily rhythms seemed so crowded and everyone always seemed so busy. How could we break that cycle and ensure a culture of reflection and planning?

Setting the pace of an organization is the fundamental responsibility of a chief executive and far too many of us have not paid enough attention to the rhythms of our organizations.

When do you eat together? When do you create space to get to know one another? When do you plan to create community?

None of these things will happen by accident but require forward planning. The best leaders know that setting a rhythm that encourages after-action project reviews, community meals, days or evenings out, silent spaces in the office, walks at lunchtime, a running club, regularly stopping to celebrate success and having enough spaces where people can retreat and recover after a time of busy activity is vital to success, creativity, innovation and perspective.

Millennial leaders create organizations that are organic; that have space to breathe.

CONNECTING WITH YOUR EMOTIONS

Rachel: We are looking for millennial leaders who care about us, who engage relationally, who understand the relational impact they are having through their emotions and put a high value on listening and responding to gut instinct emotions in decision making.

In our research, 'caring towards individuals' was in the top four of the characteristics seen in the best leaders.

Simon: Yet emotional constipation seems to be a British disease, and no more so than in British baby boomer/Gen X male leaders. Connecting with your emotions would be seen for these generations as a weakness; a sign that you really had lost it.

The inability to listen to your emotions has become as contagious as the common cold among leaders.

Yet the rise of emotional intelligence is addressing this and has become a vital skill for millennial leaders, whose lives are relationally centred.

There is a growing recognition that your emotions are 'good data' when facing decisions and that the ability to read other people's emotions is vital in steering the course for organizations in a rapidly changing and dynamic environment.

But how, as a millennial leader, do you learn to *really* listen to your emotions?

And how does that work in the midst of a strategy decision when you have five strategies in front of you and you need to decide which one to go with?

Or you have three great candidates for promotion that you're finding it difficult to decide between?

Or your most destructive emotions are rising in a crisis situation and are in danger of taking over in an unhelpful way?

It comes from listening to your gut: that's data too. It's data that comes from the wealth of life experience, good and bad, that you have had. Wouldn't you want all your life experience to be brought to bear on your decisions?

How many times after the event have you heard a leader say, 'If only I'd trusted my gut instinct . . . if only I'd listened to my inner voice . . . if only I'd trusted that bad feeling that I had . . .'?

I have made some bad hiring decisions in my time and, with the majority of them, I knew there was something not quite right at the time of hiring but couldn't quite put my finger on it.

On one occasion, I had just an inkling through reading someone's body language of a bad attitude towards women and, again, I failed to trust my inner emotions and made a bad decision.

So how do you let your emotional brain have a more equal input into decisions alongside your rational brain? It starts with being self-observant.

In my experience, the most emotionally intelligent leaders journal, especially journaling about their emotions.

The benefits of keeping a journal have been well documented and include

- a greater level of self-awareness;
- a greater ability to process information;
- a greater ability to process emotions;
- an increased ability to remember information;
- an increased ability to reflect on situations.

One of the techniques to enable processing is the SOLE approach:

> **S** What was the **situation** that you are processing? Who, when, what, where?
>
> **O** What did you **observe** about your behaviours, your response to the situation?
>
> **L** What did you **learn** from your engagement with the situation? What will you repeat and what won't you do again?
>
> **E** What were your **emotions**? How did you feel before, during and after the situation?

Why not give it a try?

LEARNING TO LISTEN TO AND TRUST YOUR EMOTIONS

Simon: If we are truly to listen to our emotions then, as well as journaling about them, we need to be able to listen to them in the moment:

Listen to our bodies

The more extreme the emotions, the more likely they are to have physical effects, such as

- butterflies in your stomach before a significant presentation;
- headaches after the exertion of a major activity as we come down from an adrenaline high;
- shaking with the fear of facing a specific situation;
- numbness or total exhaustion after a particularly emotional meeting.

I have experienced a number of situations that have been emotionally difficult and, in the week leading up to them, my emotions went from anger and fear to insomnia. In such situations, there are times when I need to go out and walk, times when I need to process verbally or to binge-watch a box set and times where I need to focus. Listening to our bodies and responding to what they are telling us is vitally important.

Responding appropriately is also essential and using a scale of one to ten to measure the intensity of emotions can be helpful, as well as recording the coping techniques that helped you respond previously.

In doing this, you can develop greater self-awareness, greater ability to cope and greater ability to appropriately respond. Also, it's great to be able to say, 'This is bad, but not nearly as bad as when . . .'

Give voice to your emotions and encourage others to do the same

As we have seen, authenticity is key to millennial leaders and authentically expressing our emotions and allowing others to do so in a leadership environment is a vital skill.

Having a specific moment in a team meeting when reaching a decision to ask, 'How does each one of us feel about this decision?' can be a great way of breaking the ice and getting people talking. Expressions of anxiety, fear, excitement, joy, peace and apathy should be encouraged.

If members of your team are finding it particularly hard to express their emotions, there are a number of techniques that can enable you to unlock this within them:

- Going first by expressing your own emotions about a decision, thereby giving permission to others to do the same.
- Noticing people's body language and asking questions associated with it.
- Using a simple scale of happiness about a decision, such as asking people to close their fists and then give a score from one to five with their fingers as to how happy they are with the decision being made. After a count of three, everyone reveals their fingers and there can be an increase in energy in the room to discuss how people are really feeling.

It takes leaders who are secure in their identity to allow this to happen and to not feel challenged by it. To encourage you, the emotions already exist. They will be expressed as soon as you leave the room, so you may as well give people the tools and techniques to deal with them while you're there, as they will enable new insights, new views, new perspectives.

It takes bravery and courage, but creates a more dynamic, more engaged, more motivated environment where people feel trusted, empowered and more committed to the final decision that is made.

DEVELOPING A CULTURE OF REFLECTION AND PLANNING

Simon: 'Why can't we just slow down? The pace is relentless, totally mind-blowing and unending. There's never any time to stop, to think, to reflect, to plan. Please help us.'

The cry from one millennial member of our team could have come from anywhere in the organization. The pace of restructuring, of growing, of meeting increasing donor, regulatory and global demand just wouldn't go away.

Plans were becoming more and more short term, focused on meeting the needs of this month, this week, today.

We had to create some space; some additional bandwidth for our teams. We needed to work smarter and stop burning one another out. But how?

How do you enable an organization to break out of a constant short-termism? To take a long view? To focus on the important rather than the urgent and to create the space for reflection and planning?

For millennial leaders in an always-on, globally connected world, these are critical questions.

And the simple answer is that you have to *stop*.

Stop long enough to start stopping some activities. And you need to be ruthless in doing so, to tackle some sacred cows in the organization and ask why you are really doing them.

At one point I became extremely unpopular for stopping short-term teams. At another, for closing one of our offices. Both were done with a view to simplifying what we were doing, to create space to breathe and to focus on our core purpose.

However, there are some complexities underneath this focus on stopping activities that are also worth examining.

Challenge unhealthy leadership behaviours

Sometimes the relentlessness is caused by poor leadership of a team or a department. You have a leader who is unable to manage his or her own pattern of work and is therefore incapable of helping the team to plan effectively. It becomes a downward spiral. You may need a new leader, or at least a coach who will come alongside and enable the team leader to see the investment needed, the structure and rhythm required to escape a rapidly descending spiral.

Encourage teams to ask for help

Sometimes the relentlessness is caused because lack of, or poor, planning has meant that the right resource is not available at the right time. Or perhaps events have caused that to happen.

In those moments, teams have to ask for help. And the best way to help is to put as much control as possible into their hands. Give them the budget and responsibility to hire short-term help or to recruit new skills into the team. Empower, empower, empower with the expectation of broken cycles of ferocious activity.

And if you can't afford to invest to do the job properly, it's a sure sign that you shouldn't be doing it.

Force a rhythm of intentional reflection

Ensuring that approval processes require reflection is an important step in breaking the cycle.

We ran a quarterly grants committee that would approve multi-million-pound grants to external third parties to undertake development work around the world.

It had become custom and practice before my time to approve the next multi-year grant before the previous one had finished, on the premise that there needed to be continuity of staff, continuity of action, continuity of money flows.

However, this sometimes meant that the grants committee were making decisions blind, without any formal feedback on the effectiveness of an existing programme.

So, we changed the rhythm and it had multiple positive effects. Formal reviews of ending programmes now had to be completed at least three months before the end of the programme.

First, this meant that partners worked harder in the earlier years of a programme and there was less running around at the last minute to complete activities.

Second, all new programmes were assessed against solid results from the previous programme. Approvals for programmes fell by 25 per cent, and 90 per cent of future programmes ended up being adjusted in scale and scope in response to feedback from past activities. But that was a good thing.

We were finally focused on ensuring that we reflected on previous results; that we took the time to reflect on current practice and to adjust what we were doing rather than ploughing on regardless.

Learning from experience, one millennial leader explained the need for leaders to draw healthy boundaries for themselves and their organizations:

Sometimes you just need to stop. There's always more you can do, and learning what you can do and when you should say no can be challenging, as is learning how you draw the boundaries when you've got to lead lots of other people.

How are you, as a millennial leader, encouraging a deep level of insight for yourself and for your organization?

THE MARKS OF A MILLENNIAL LEADER

Simon: In summary, here again are the four marks of a millennial leader that we've explored:

Mark 1: Millennial leaders are secure in their identity, have dealt with their fears, have learnt to be vulnerable and lead out of who they are.

Mark 2: Millennial leaders have a strong moral compass, are able to articulate their core values and beliefs and have developed the discipline of aligning their decisions and actions with those beliefs.

Mark 3: Millennial leaders have developed an inner strength through establishing rhythms of life that enable them to persevere and bounce back, whatever is thrown at them.

Mark 4: Millennial leaders have developed a deep insight, by creating space for perspective, reflection and planning and enabling themselves and their teams to connect with their emotions.

Now we move on to look at Mark 5: influence. This one deserves a whole part of the book to itself.

You can check how you are doing in all these areas by taking the Forge Leadership Five 'I's test online at <www.millennial-leader. com/health-checks/>.

Part three

FORGING THE FUTURE – HOW MILLENNIALS ARE STARTING TO LEAD WITH INFLUENCE

INTRODUCTION TO PART THREE

Simon: Imagine trying to learn to windsurf without the benefit of having watched a YouTube video first or without the guidance of someone who has done it before.

It would no doubt be very funny to watch you have a go!

You would probably take a number of attempts to put the sail on to the board (it's more complicated that it looks) and even more attempts to stand upright on it.

Chances are you would give up very quickly having got wet, cold and slightly embarrassed in the process.

There is a way that windsurfing works, a technique and approach that will maximize the potential for your success. There is a poise, a set of tools and approaches that have been learnt and need to be passed on.

Part three of this book seeks to help you get up on the board, grab the sail and start surfing. We don't want you to fall into the water continuously, because each fall has an impact on the windsurfer and those who follow behind.

So, consider Part three a guide full of concrete, practical steps that will enable millennial leaders to lean into their unique skills, core beliefs and gifting, to bring transformation in the culture of business and change the rules of the game through their influence, allowing everyone to win.

Chapter nine

TRANSFORMING INFLUENCE

Simon: I was 37 when I become CEO of a £25 million turnover charity. In 2019, the oldest millennial is now 35. So, what kind of influence are millennial leaders having today?

THE INFLUENCE MILLENNIAL LEADERS ARE HAVING TODAY

Simon: The Message Trust is a Christian Youth Charity based in Manchester. It has over one hundred and ten employees and the average age is 27. The UK leadership team is primarily formed of millennials.

In 2018, they came first in the *Sunday Times* 'Top 100 non-profits to work for' poll. The annual poll questions employees on a range of factors and it is the employees who determine the results. In their write-up of why The Message Trust had won this coveted and celebrated award, the *Sunday Times* reported:

> A former heroin addict with a criminal record, Joe Rogers couldn't hold down a job until he started working for The Message Trust last June as an apprentice chef in its social enterprise the Mess Café.

> 'It has transformed my life,' says the 32-year-old, who was brought up by alcoholic parents and saw his eldest brother die from an overdose. 'I love coming into work. You can't really have a bad day here because everybody is so positive,' says Rogers . . .

> The 115 employees of the trust, which takes music and drama into schools and works in local communities and prisons from

its six UK hubs, say it has a strong social conscience (97% positive) and is run on strong values (96%). Both are top question scores, two of the 28 it achieved. It ranked first for the Leadership, My Manager, Personal Growth, Giving Something Back and My Team categories.

After break-ins and vandalism by workers at the clothing factory he ran with his brother, chief executive Andy Hawthorne founded the organization in 1992 to spread the Christian message in schools across Manchester through dance band the World Wide Message Tribe.

'Initially it was just a band reaching marginalized youth but when you go into a community you realize there is so much need in communities,' he says.

Laura Wilding, a stylist at the organization's social enterprise Shine Hair and Beauty, has just qualified as a barber and is given time off once a week to do a computer course. 'They are investing in my future,' says former drug addict Wilding, who joined five years ago after leaving rehab. 'The first thing that struck me was how much of a family it is,' says Wilding . . .

Colleagues care about one another (92%, first) and have fun at work (91%, second). Managers are supportive too, caring about employees as individuals (90%, first) and how satisfied they are in their work (88%, first). Mission team members typically earn £19,500 and perks include a contributory pension and staff discounts but rewards go far beyond the pay packet. Work is an important part of life for employees (93%, first), who wouldn't leave tomorrow to work anywhere else (84%, second).[1]

As I read the book, *Being the Message: Lessons Learned on the Frontline of Mission* by Andy Hawthorne, Carl Beech and Friends, which seeks to encapsulate the success factors behind the organization, a number of elements were striking:

1 The commitment to the cause and purpose (keeping mission hot, keeping prayer hot and loving the urban poor).
2 The commitment to one another (taking responsibility, mates on a mission).
3 The commitment to humility (don't take yourself too seriously, and realize that leading always requires you to go lower in serving others).
4 The energy and vitality (it's all about passion; remember the power of multiplication; think like an entrepreneur; believe the problem can become the solution).

It is clear that The Message Trust has a huge transforming influence in the lives of young people. So, how can millennial leaders emulate that and build cultures that are similarly transformative?

Chapter ten

TRANSFORMING CULTURE

Simon: There is a growing recognition that transforming culture is the main task of a leader.

> The dynamics of culture and leadership cannot be separated. In fact, one can argue that the only thing of real importance that leaders do is create and manage culture and the unique talent of leaders is their ability to understand and work with culture. The ability to initiate and sustain positive cultural changes may prove to be the single greatest need of twenty-first century organization.
>
> Edgar H. Schein[1]

MILLENNIAL LEADERS: HOW TO TRANSFORM CULTURE

Simon: A question I often get asked is, 'How can I, as a millennial leader, work together with others to foster an environment and culture where millennials can truly prosper and in a way that is also good for my organization?'

In a recent conversation with a millennial leader, we were having exactly that discussion. Faced with low staff engagement, high staff turnover and an inability to attract, retain and motivate millennial workers and leaders, our focus turned to helping her change the environment of her business.

My first piece of advice was to bring together a group of millennial leaders with the senior team. The second was to draw up 19 practical, proven ways in which she could start today to map out the future and create momentum in her business, working hand in hand across the generations.

I would like to share those practical tools with you now. They are tools that I have used personally as I have helped organizations make the transition from old leadership approaches to new leadership approaches. They are ideas that can bring the generations together to drive lasting change.

Think of these tools as the 'kit' that every windsurfer needs: a great board, strong sails, a wetsuit that fits. They are the keys to ensuring that you can ride the waves and harness the wind.

Each of the tools is designed to move you from an old to a new leadership approach. Table 10.1 will help you identify which tools you need to apply to transform your leadership in a specific area. The bracketed numbers in the 'tools' column relate to the further explorations of each one provided in the main text.

Table 10.1 Tools for change for the millennial leader

What has worked previously	What works now	Tools to enable you to respond
Lead from what you do	Lead from who you are	Harness proximity (1) Harness directness (2)
Create environments where you win	Create environments where everyone wins	Harness collaboration (5)
Celebrate the individual	Celebrate the team	Harness collaboration (5)
Win at work/lose at home	Win everywhere	Harness whole-life flourishing (4)

(continued)

Table 10.1 (*continued*)

What has worked previously	*What works now*	*Tools to enable you to respond*
Create a flexible environment	Develop a sense of community	Harness community (6)
Business is good for the shareholders	Business is good for employees, community and shareholders	Harness shared purpose (18) Harness better ethos and values (12)
Total commitment to work	Total commitment to life	Harness whole-life flourishing (4)
Lead from the top down	Lead from anywhere	Harness leading from anywhere (7)
Use data to prove everything and create a grand plan	Go with your gut and experiment	Harness creativity (14) Harness experimentation (17) Harness curiosity (16)
Good ideas come from a small number of people	Good ideas can come from anywhere and anyone	Harness diversity (15) Harness creativity (14)
You need to have a career plan	Flexibility, moving around, getting great experience of work and life	Harness agility (8)
Feedback on performance from one person once a year	Feedback on performance from anyone at any time	Harness directness (2) Harness proximity (1) Harness a feedback culture (19)
Business is a series of transactions	Business is a series of relationships	Harness directness (2) Harness proximity (1) Harness collaboration (5)

(*continued*)

Table 10.1 (*continued*)

What has worked previously	What works now	Tools to enable you to respond
The end justifies the means	Integrity is everything	Harness directness (2) Harness proximity (1) Harness the breaking down of stigma (10)
Leadership is power	Leadership is service	Harness understanding and respect across generations (3) Harness fairness (11) Harness the breaking down of stigma (10)
Winning in the short term	Win for the long term	Harness shared purpose (18) Harness preparedness for Gen Z (13)
No point in developing people when they move on so quickly and have no commitment	We need to develop the next generation now	Harness a two-way mentoring and coaching culture (9)
Drive people with targets	Inspire people with purpose	Harness shared purpose (18)
Leaders need to be guarded and measured	Leaders need to be open, vulnerable and transparent	Harness directness (2) Harness proximity (1)
The winner has the greatest market share this year	The winner is still here when we are all gone	Harness shared purpose (18) Harness preparedness for Gen Z (13)

If you are unsure which areas you need to work on, then the diagnostic tools at <www.millennial-leader.com/health-checks/> will pinpoint these specifically for you.

Out of the 20 leadership approaches come 19 tools for change. Let's take these tools in turn and identify why each one is important, why it's a problem that needs solving, why there's conflict and what you can do about it.

1 Harness proximity
Why it's important
Millennials want authenticity and relational engagement.

Why it's a problem
This can be a problem for millennial leaders in particular. Although relational to the core, millennials often lack confidence, and the fear of rejection and need for approval can stifle proximity.

Why there's conflict
Older leaders tend to be more guarded and protective and less likely to be vulnerable.

What to do about it
In short, it's about being more human; more of yourself. The solution is to implement everything we talked about in the 'Identity' and 'Integrity' sections of Part two.

Harnessing proximity can include building rhythms of eating together as part of the working week, walking together, playing sport and socializing together. It can also mean looking at patterns of work to allow space for employee engagement.

One of the complaints I heard most often from employees about their bosses was, 'I just don't get time with them'.

2 Harness directness
Why it's important
Millennials want real and direct communication and open, honest dialogue in the context of relationship.

Why it's a problem
This requires bravery and courage from a millennial leader and the willingness to be vulnerable. It also requires a breaking away from the attitude that employees are 'children' who are to be looked after and from the 'false responsibility' that can be taken on to protect, support, guide and provide security.

Why there's conflict
Among older leaders, views of leadership tend to be more authoritarian and communication more guarded and on a 'need to know' basis.

What to do about it
Directness needs to be cultivated in one-to-one communication. This can only happen as leaders become more self-aware and more secure in their own identity, and then encourage and model for those working for them a style of working that is direct, fair, humble and authentic. Again, the 'Identity' and 'Integrity' sections from Part two are great places to start with this.

Organizational decisions need to be taken to open up decision-making and planning processes to include more employees and to take more risks in treating employees as trusted partners in the organization.

3 Harness understanding and respect across generations
Why it's important
We've demonstrated the significant conflict and different world views that exist across the generations. In this context, dialogue between the generations is more vital than ever.

Why it's a problem
There is diversity in each generation. This book has been about trends and, as good an indicator as they are, they are really only that: an indicator. There is huge diversity of behaviour and attitude among the vibrant and dynamic millennial generation.

Why there's conflict
Stereotyping and misunderstanding have caused tension. World view and approach changes have caused conflict.

What to do about it
There is no substitute for actually sitting down with the people you manage and asking them great questions. After all, you are a human being, a unique person with a unique set of skills, attributes, behaviours and world views, and the people around you are not a stereotype from their generation either.

So ask questions such as:

- How can I create an environment in which you can flourish?
- What would motivate you to higher levels of performance?
- What is it about the way I manage you that you would like to change?
- Who have you seen leading in a way that really inspires you?

4 Harness whole-life flourishing
Why it's important
Our research has shown the importance to millennials of whole-life flourishing and they will only thrive working for leaders who take that seriously.

Why it's a problem
Millennials are struggling to find the right balance between work and life, often with blurred boundaries between the two.

Why there's conflict
The changing nature of commitment in the workplace has led to different expectations across the generations.

What to do about it
More and more employers are finding ways to enable employees to have a richer experience of work. Whether that is a secondment overseas, a sabbatical to serve on a disaster response, a career break to complete studies, a bursary to study or a gym in the workplace.

From two and a half hours a week to go to the gym in work time, to completely flexible schedules, to extended parental leave, to hours off to study, this is led by a greater focus on performance and deliverables than on hours worked.

It has become much more the norm to spread your hours so that you can pick up the children on certain days from school, to work part-time or to have hours that extend into the evenings or weekends to allow partners to work parallel schedules in order to care for children.

The benefits to business include increased staff retention and motivation.

This requires millennial leaders to have greater levels of trust in their employees and to think differently about what employees want. However, the results can be remarkable in terms of the ability to attract and retain employees.

5 Harness collaboration
Why it's important
Throughout the research, millennials consistently shared that collaboration is a key to a good working environment and is seen

as an extremely positive contribution to the way we are going to lead.

Why it's a problem
Many millennials see the scale of the challenges facing humanity in a sharper way than any generation before them. They also see the diversity and creativity of their generation and are much less likely to put up with narrow organizational visions that are not partnership focused and collaborative in nature.

Why there's conflict
Older leaders and generations can often see more to lose from collaboration than gain and have sometimes had very negative experiences of collaboration in the past.

What to do about it
With limited resources, it's important to know which projects most benefit from collaboration:

- Projects where the task and vision are greater than can be achieved by an individual organization.
- Projects where substantial behaviour change in the mass market is needed.
- Projects involving volatile and uncertain circumstances where the risk and reward can be shared.
- Projects where there are existing players who have sub-optimal skills and resources.

Whether collaboration is at an individual, team, project or organizational level, from my experience the following attitudes and abilities are required by every participant to enable collaboration to work well:

- A willingness to share success.
- An ability to act fairly.
- A high level of willingness to be honest and direct.
- A high level of interest in and commitment to the collaboration topic.
- A high level of inquisitiveness and willingness to think creatively about solutions.
- A high level of ability to listen.

6 Harness community
Why it's important
One of the remarkable things for us throughout the research interviews was the extremely high value put on the quality of relationships in the workplace. The best places to work were explained purely in terms of the team there, the people being great and a sense of collaboration and community.

Why it's a problem
In contrast, the worst places were explained as places where the relationships just didn't seem to work; where people were not interested in your whole self or relating outside work tasks.

Why there's conflict
For previous generations, work was work and community was community. The shift to building communities at work (where we have to be 'professional') is challenging for many.

What to do about it
Community can be easier to harness in young, dynamic organizations who are growing and entrepreneurial, and where the workplace often feels like family. This can also be more easily discovered in non-profits and faith-based communities. It can be harder to encourage within larger, more established organizations,

where growth has brought a loss of shared purpose, loss of sense of belonging and a loss of heart and hope.

Community though can be rediscovered and often it's the small things that matter.

- It's the proximity of leaders that enables them to be real and authentic.
- It's the developing of a shared sense of purpose.
- It's the journeying through the hard times collectively.
- It's the openness and transparency harnessed by leaders with a strong sense of identity.
- It's the individual care that is shown to members of staff.

7 Harness leading from anywhere
Why it's important
Our research demonstrated that, for many millennials, leadership is something that is not confined to certain people. People in any position can be of influence and therefore lead. For us, leadership is all about influence: influencing those around us positively from wherever we find ourselves within an organizational hierarchy or society.

Why it's a problem
Today, you need so much more than just a title to make you a leader. Titles can be useful for structure and empowerment, but leaders of character, secure in their identity, resilient and full of integrity can rise from anywhere and do not need a title to lead.

Why there's conflict
Older leaders tend to be more hierarchal in nature and outlook.

What to do about it

So, how can you harness leadership from anywhere and not see it as a threat? Try

1 to encourage the plethora of ideas and creativity and give them space to breathe;
2 to find a fund of resources and time to encourage people to experiment with ideas from anywhere in the organization;
3 to remove the barriers for people to act and encourage a culture of getting on and doing it;
4 to applaud those who have the courage to take a risk, take action and address issues. Celebrate them.

Seth Godin believes that now is our time. In *Tribes: We Need You to Lead Us*, he argues that:

> the barriers to leadership have fallen. There are tribes everywhere, many in search of leaders. Which creates a dilemma for you: Without a barrier, why not begin? No-one gives you permission or approval or a permit to lead. You can just do it. The only one who can say no is you.[2]

8 Harness agility

Why it's important

There is increasing volatility and uncertainty in the environment. Millennials tend to be more optimistic and more adaptable when it comes to new technologies and approaches. We are digital natives, so we are much more likely to envisage ways of working that creatively use new technology platforms, content and processes that would have seemed impossible a decade ago.

Why it's a problem

We want to do a great job and we want to do it with the best technology and processes available, but many of our organizations are 30 years behind in their thinking. Being aware of the generational shift in technology competence and understanding is important and it means that engaging millennials in the early stages of system design is vital if organizations are to stay ahead of the curve and keep millennials motivated.

Why there's conflict

Businesses can get stuck in proven ways of doing things that have always worked and think themselves immune from the changing environment.

What to do about it

In a study of organizations they were working with to increase agility, McKinsey and Co. looked at the differences between 'bureaucratic' and 'agile' organizations on a number of parameters, both stable and dynamic, and found the largest gaps in points on the following indicators:

(a) rapid iteration and experimentation
(b) technology, systems and tools
(c) continual learning
(d) sensing and seizing opportunities
(e) role mobility
(f) information transparency
(g) flexible resource allocation
(h) performance orientation
(i) active partnerships and ecosystem
(j) open physical and virtual environment.[3]

In addition to these I would add creativity, diversity, directness, harnessing leadership from anywhere and harnessing proximity as key parameters to focus on when looking at harnessing agility in an organization.

More than anything, though, hiring for attitude as opposed to talent is a critical factor in creating agility and momentum towards a more flexible organization. Factors to consider when hiring for attitude on flexibility include

- the ability to consider diverse viewpoints;
- speed of adaptation when new information is introduced;
- an attitude of continuous learning;
- an ability to sense and seize new opportunities;
- an ability to create wide networks and partnerships;
- an ability to create and operate in open systems.

9 Harness a two-way mentoring and coaching culture
Why it's important
Millennials put a high value on mentoring and coaching. We have much to learn from older generations, but much to share as well.

Why it's a problem
Of millennials, 57 per cent regarded their mentoring experience as 'very effective', which leaves quite a bit of room for the effectiveness to be increased.

Why there's conflict
Mentoring and coaching is generally seen as one way (older to younger).

What to do about it
One of the most widely cited, successful examples of transforming culture is to encourage reverse mentoring as a way to connect our different generations within the workplace and prepare us as millennials to lead.

This is a mentor partnership between senior mentor and a younger, millennial mentee who exchange knowledge and expertise.

This is the creation of a bridge across which information, knowledge and experience flow both ways.

While the older colleague hopes to develop the millennial's leadership skills, the millennial has the opportunity to update their mentor's knowledge of technology and the millennial generation. This has been seen as extremely successful and is widely documented.[4] [5] [6]

Hugh Osgood, a leader in his seventies, speaks much wisdom:

> If a senior leader is being authentic with a younger leader, the senior leader can gain so much from that younger leader. People have got to stop thinking of it as one-way traffic. You know the kind of attitude: 'I'm the superhero who is giving to you'.[7]

The reality is younger leaders can give to older leaders and vice versa. We all need to realize that we're on a journey.

10 Harness the breaking down of stigma
Why it's important
Breaking down stigma in the workplace is vital for millennial leaders. It begins with examining our own attitudes and asking ourselves where we are creating cultures that continue to support behaviours, attitudes and actions that promote stigma, whether around faith, disability, mental health, race, gender or sexuality.

Why it's a problem
Millennials have a strong belief in the inclusion of everyone and in the rights of everyone to a safe and secure place, without stigmatization, that enables full flourishing.

Why there's conflict
These can be difficult subjects to talk about in the workplace and ones that often challenge deeply held prejudices and ingrained behaviours.

What to do about it
Jane Magree, Risk Advisory Partner at Deloitte, gives three ways in which leaders can break down stigma associated with one significant stigma of our time, mental health:

Beginning to have unvarnished conversations about depression, anxiety and mental health.

Increasing the help seeking options for people and effectively communicating these.

Supporting people and caregivers facing mental health challenges by actively building communities at work that support people.[8]

Many employers are responding in positive ways and the launch of peer-to-peer support networks is one approach that is providing non-judgemental, supportive environments in which honesty can replace silence and in which it's 'OK not to be OK'.

11 Harness fairness
Why it's important
Earlier, we saw how fairness is a core belief of millennials. Ranging from eliminating gender-biased pay to speaking up on behalf of those who have been the victims of power in the past, millennials have been championing responses to human trafficking, supporting the living wage and advocating for fairness in the workplace.

Why it's a problem
Millennials are actively looking for leaders who harness fairness, who have an innate ability to utilize power for good.

Why there's conflict
Millennials have developed a skill of exposing those misusing power, developed through observing the scandals of historic sexual abuse,

scams and fraud and experiencing the pain of seeing our futures negatively shaped by the collapse of the banking system in 2008.

What to do about it

This starts with having an awareness of the power that you actually have as a leader. I remember one of my bosses saying to me, 'Simon, you have to realize that, once you are a leader, everyone is watching you. Like it or not, they are watching your every move. They watch you when you come in in the morning: are you grumpy, happy or measured? Are you secure, stable or erratic? Are you wielding power, reserving power or giving away power?'

The best leaders I have followed use their power generously. They are generous in their humour, in their praise, with their time, in sponsoring and supporting your development, in giving away power and seeing others prosper.

How ready are you to be generous with the power you have as a leader, recognizing it as a gift that needs to keep on giving until everyone is treated fairly, everyone has the same chance of promotion, everyone has the opportunity to flourish, everyone has the opportunity to shine regardless of class or background and purely on merit?

12 Harness better ethos and values

Why it's important

We have seen how important it is for millennials to be aligned with the ethos and values of the organization in which they are working and how this increases the likelihood that we will stay in a business for longer and be more committed to it.

Why it's a problem

We have already noted that turnover rates and burnout levels among millennials are at record levels.

Why there's conflict
The ethos and values of the millennial generation have shifted dramatically and organizations need to examine their own ethos and values in that light if they are to prosper.

What to do about it
You may already have an ethos and values statement. It's something that's been in focus for over a decade and most organizations have recognized the benefit of articulating the 'how' as well as the 'what' and 'why'. However, have you ever dialogued these with your younger leaders?

The ethics and value bases of the millennial generation have been shaped differently. And soon, we will be the majority of employees in the workplace.

Creating an environment in which the ethos and values of organizations are examined not only in the light of the ethos and values that millennials are identifying with, but also of the core beliefs that they are now articulating, will generate positive engagement and energy.

If you are ready and willing to embrace a move in your values towards more transparency, more authenticity, more grace, more relationship focus, more purpose, more passion, more diversity and more mutual respect and understanding, then get ready for a values-based revolution and higher levels of engagement from millennials.

13 Harness preparedness for Gen Z
Why it's important
When we asked what the best thing about leading is, the vast majority of millennials intuitively responded that it's investing in the next generation; seeing others develop, grow and flourish.

In fact, leadership was defined as taking others with us and developing them in such a way that they can replace us and go further than we can. Often, the best places of work were so called due to a culture of developing others. Equally, those named the worst placed no value on developing and growing individuals outside a job specification.

Why it's a problem
It's not. It's a great opportunity.

Why there's conflict
There is no way that this would have been the best thing about my (Simon's) leadership in my twenties and early thirties. I was far too focused on making an impact and a difference myself, on sorting out how this all worked and what my part in it was. My world was much too narrow and hadn't expanded enough to give me the perspective to think about what was coming next. Older leaders need assistance in working this shift of emphasis through.

What to do about it
This is a massive and very welcome shift in focus and attention. It exemplifies the servant-hearted, long-term and sustainable focus that millennials have and needs to be encouraged in every organization by giving millennial leaders time and space to mentor those younger than they are.

14 Harness creativity
Why it's important
Millennial leaders know that creativity is vital to long-term success.

Why it's a problem
Creative ideas require space and time to be planted, to germinate and be cared for so that they can come to fruition.

Why there's conflict
Creatives often feel misunderstood, as if they are viewed as impractical, random and not focused on the immediate needs of the business.

What to do about it
New approaches include creating an 'incubator' in an organization where new ideas are put into a 'greenhouse' of testing and growth and where they are protected for a time from the current parameters the business uses to measure success.

Managing the risk of the investments being made across a broad portfolio of incubated projects that are ranked from low risk to high risk can enable a business to incubate a significant number of projects at one time, while managing the exposure of the business.

Other businesses have successfully applied the technique of agile software development to create 'scrums': short-term teams located in the same place for a fixed period of time in close formation to develop a specific idea, with the expectation that it may or may not succeed.

15 Harness diversity
Why it's important
The days of mono-ethnic, monocultural businesses are limited, if not over. Most of us work in multicultural, multi-ethnic teams, whether they are geographically confined to the UK or we are part of globally connected, globally integrated cross-cultural teams.

Why it's a problem
The work to become truly multi-ethnic and multicultural is far from over. A further generational shift is required to enable all organizations to embrace this fully and wholeheartedly at all levels.

Why there's conflict

Older leaders have often become comfortable within their own class, gender and ethnicity. Breaking out of this can be challenging because often, with these have come success and power.

What to do about it

Training for staff on working cross-culturally and embracing diversity has become essential. As millennials build globally connected, multi-ethnic, multicultural teams, enabled by technology, travel and a globally accessible market, the need to help teams understand the different approaches and cultural norms becomes more and more vital.

Erin Meyer, in her wonderful book, *The Culture Map*, describes it like this:

> Leaders have always needed to understand human nature and personality differences to be successful in business – that's nothing new. What's new is the requirement for twenty-first century leaders to be prepared to understand a wider, richer array of work styles than ever before and to be able to determine what aspects of an interaction are simply a result of personality and which are a result of differences in cultural perspective.[9]

Leaders therefore need to work hard

- to educate themselves;
- to engage themselves in immersive cross-cultural experiences;
- to refuse to take the lazy path of building teams 'like them';
- to build social interactions that are culturally diverse to aid understanding;
- to create the capacity and competency to look through cultural lenses.

16 Harness curiosity
Why it's important
Millennial leaders are committed life-long learners and bring a curiosity and challenge to business problem-solving.

Why it's a problem
The curiosity and challenge can often be perceived as disloyalty or a challenge to authority.

Why there's conflict
Older leaders can perceive curiosity as arrogance and are not as used to being challenged and questioned.

What to do about it
Great leaders harness curiosity in their teams by

- encouraging them to expand their horizons;
- focusing on the quality of interaction among their teams;
- encouraging great questions;
- asking great questions;
- practising continual learning themselves.

Here are some great questions you can ask to engage your team in developing their approach to curiosity.

(a) How do other people do this?
(b) Who are the best people in the world at doing this and how and why do they do it that way?
(c) I don't understand. What's the best explanation we have?
(d) Whom do we know who can give us a better handle on this?
(e) How did you come to that conclusion?
(f) Tell me what your process was in coming to that result?

(g) What other options did you look at and why did you dismiss them?

(h) What would be the opposite of the approach you are suggesting?

(i) What would this look like if we started with a blank piece of paper?

(j) What have we learnt from taking this approach?

17 Harness experimentation
Why it's important
Millennial leaders want to create environments where their teams can come up with bright, innovative ideas and a culture where the best ideas triumph.

Why it's a problem
This requires safe environments in which teams can experiment and learn from failure. The research tells us that millennial leaders have a fear of failure.

Why there's conflict
Different generational attitudes towards risk; older leaders' tendency to operate from gut instinct and experience and the tension between these.

What to do about it
Encourage the use of testing and data: The standard approach is to use data to develop optimum ways of working or a best practice approach that can be rolled out across a large organization. The increase in the pace of change means that this is rapidly becoming an outmoded approach. Instead, focus on creating organisms in your organization that continually learn, by asking:

- What did we learn from that last test? Therefore, what can we apply to this next piece of work to optimize it?

- Is that piece of learning still valid now or do we need to revisit all our assumptions?

Leaders therefore need to be encouraged not to jump to conclusions too quickly (something we are prone to do) and not to hold on to their experience too tightly (something we are even more likely to do), but to let the tests speak for themselves.

Make learning from failure a goal: How about putting into someone's objectives that they must fail at least once over the next year and be able to explain the lessons they learned from that failure?

The trouble with wanting a learning organization is that, often, we want an academic learning organization rather than a practical learning one. We want the success without the mess.

Encourage diverse thinking: You can develop diverse thinking by always insisting that people present to you at least nine ideas that they considered and threw away before coming to the idea or solution they are now presenting.

This requires emphasizing to leaders the thinking process and the analysis process and being rigorous in maintaining a decision-making posture that likes alternatives.

Build research and testing into every programme: It's always amazing to me how many organizations don't bother doing research into their audiences, customers and products and how little testing really happens in practice. My experience is that this is usually driven by delivery programmes that are overambitious and time-scales that are constantly being reduced.

18 Harness shared purpose
Why it's important
Millennials don't want to work because they are told to but want to understand the 'why' behind it and see how their actions will have an impact and make a difference. They also want to join in with the development of the evolutionary purpose of the organization and be able to influence it.

Why it's a problem
Most organizations ask employees to join them in delivering the existing purpose of the organization, which is set and stationary. Millennials want a say in the evolving purpose.

Why there's conflict
Many older leaders don't think in terms of their organizations being living, breathing, organic entities.

What to do about it
Frederic Laloux in his book, *Reinventing Organizations*, explores how organizations can listen to their purpose and encourage staff to think in terms of the organization as a breathing and living entity whose purpose is developed and evolves. He suggests a number of exercises that can help an organization develop in this way, including 'The empty chair'.

The empty chair
A simple, less esoteric practice to listen in to an organization's purpose consists of allocating an empty chair at every meeting to represent the organization and its evolutionary purpose. Anybody participating in the meeting can, at any time, change seats, to listen to and become the voice of the organization. Here are some questions one might tune into while sitting in that chair:

1. Have the decisions and the discussion served you (the organization) well?
2. How are you at the end of this meeting?
3. What stands out to you from today's meeting?
4. In what direction do you want to go?
5. At what speed?
6. Are we being bold enough? Too bold?
7. Is there something else that needs to be said or discussed?[10]

19 Harness a feedback culture

Why it's important

The majority of millennials interviewed in our research spoke very positively about feedback in their workplace when it was regular and easy to access.

Why it's a problem

Millennials want to be adaptive and change in a fast-moving environment, but many are hampered by lack of access to frequent, focused, honest and specific feedback.

Why there's conflict

Many older leaders have been trained in systems such as yearly appraisals and have not been developed in the area of giving instantaneous, open feedback. Performance-related pay systems also inhibit this.

What to do about it

Harness an environment of safety and trust: We have already looked at the need to create environments that are relational, direct and that harness proximity. This is vital in looking at feedback as they engender places where it's safe to talk about emotions. And safe places are vital when ensuring good feedback so that it's OK to say, 'No, I don't want to give you feedback.'

Engender balance: The 80:20 rule is a good one. Strive to give feedback that is positive on four things before giving constructive feedback on change. Start slowly and be clear about what you're beginning to do. Also, start small, maybe with things that don't matter too much, instead of waiting for that big project and then laying into all that went wrong.

It's also important to praise effort as well as ability. People may have put in high levels of work but, through no fault of their own, events may have conspired against them to produce a less than brilliant outcome. The effort still went in.

Giving feedback to a team or in a team setting can be a great way to start small as well. Recently, I led a five-day leadership workshop with CEO-level leaders and I tried a technique out on them that I've used before. And I remembered how effective it really is. All you do is ask a group of people to rate from one to five how effective the meeting/event/course they have just completed was. They rate it by simply holding out their clenched fist and, after a count of three, releasing the number of fingers that tallies with their score.

Immediately, as the meeting leader, you have feedback on your performance, you know who is struggling or has struggled with the meeting and can facilitate conversations to that end.

Make it normal: It's important to integrate feedback into the daily and weekly routine, to include team feedback as well as individual feedback and to concentrate on feedback within areas that make everyone's lives easier and better. Everyone wants to make life easier and better, so it's usually easier to elicit people's honest views on these areas.

Walk the talk: Certainly tell people you are trying to get better at receiving and giving feedback. This in itself will generate conversation, often humorous. Be transparent in making it an ongoing goal that you are working towards. And don't forget to ask for feedback for yourself!

TRANSFORMING CULTURE

Simon: The 19 areas we have highlighted have described some great tools that millennials and non-millennials can start working with together to begin to transform the cultures of organizations.

They also provide a guideline for assessing your organization's readiness to support millennial leaders. We have produced an online diagnostic tool so that you can immediately tell how your organization is doing against these 19 barometers of cultural transformation. You can find it at <www.millennial-leader.com/health-checks/>.

LEADING – THE MILLENNIAL WAY

Simon: Whether you are a millennial leader, a leader of millennials or an older leader seeking to lead the millennial way, we hope this book has helped you catch the vision of a generation.

It's a vision of businesses in which

1 there is an evolving sense of inspiring purpose that aligns with our purposes as individuals;
2 there are environments where everyone wins;
3 there is an environment of fair play;
4 customers, employers and shareholders are successful;
5 there are strong, mutually beneficial relationships;

6 there is a powerful sense of unity;

7 good ideas can come from anywhere and anyone;

8 there is a commitment to integrity;

9 we all win in the long term;

10 the winner is still here when we are all gone.

It's a vision of businesses led by leaders who

1 know who they are and lead from that;

2 celebrate teams;

3 win at home and away;

4 have a total commitment to life;

5 lead from anywhere;

6 go with their gut and experiment;

7 are flexible, move around and gain great experience of work and life;

8 give and receive feedback from anyone at anytime;

9 are motivated by service;

10 develop the next generation;

11 are open, vulnerable and transparent;

12 are authentic and full of integrity.

Chapter eleven

A FINAL CHALLENGE - TO FINISH WELL

Simon: Many of the leaders interviewed as part of our research are just starting out in their leadership. Many others reading this book will have been leading for years. Regardless of where you are in your journey of leading 'the millennial way', it's important to not only start well, but *finish* well.

How many people do you see around you finishing well? I see lots of people starting well, but I also see many casualties on the way, with people stumbling over finances, pride, sexual temptation, the abuse of power, emotional and psychological wounding, critical family issues and simply failing to grow.

The World Economic Forum's 2015 survey of the leadership inspirations of 1,000 20- to 30-year-olds from more than 125 countries is telling. Pope Francis, Nelson Mandela, Mahatma Gandhi and Steve Jobs all featured in the top ten.[1] Leaders who last the distance are inspiring.

A lesser known example of a long-lasting leader is George C. Seward, a lawyer and Senior Counsel who kept working as a practising attorney until the day he died aged 101 in 2012. When asked on his 100th birthday why he kept working, he replied that there was so much more left to do and so many human rights violations still to be put right. Besides, he was having so much fun doing it, why would he stop? In his role as Chairman of the Bar Association in New York, he championed the cause of those who have no voice and he left an enduring legacy. He finished well.[2]

Of course, if you are to finish well, you have to continue well, so here are six of the necessities Professor Bobby Clinton[3] lists as being fundamental to leaders who finish well.

1 Have a **broad perspective** from which to interpret ongoing activity. Leaders who finish well consistently broaden their horizons.
2 Have an expectancy for **renewal** repeatedly. Leaders who finish well consistently seek renewal.
3 The practice of **disciplines**. Leaders who finish well remain disciplined and keep a healthy rhythm to their lives right to the end.
4 Have a **learning** posture. Leaders who finish well have a continual learning posture and maintain their curiosity for a lifetime.
5 Have **mentors**. Leaders who finish well surround themselves with mentors who hold them accountable, speak into their lives and to whom they are answerable on a long-term basis.
6 Have a singular **unique contribution**. Leaders who finish well focus on the one thing that is their unique contribution, be that the liberation of a nation, ministry to the poor or making people's lives better through technology.

After all, life is a marathon, not a sprint . . .

When my wife, Heather, decided to run the marathon aged 40, having never run before, she was inspired by a recent trip to California where she found herself running along Malibu beach with the LA Leggers. Coming back and training through the winter in Suffolk wasn't quite the same, but one thing she did learn was the technique of running for nine minutes, then walking for one minute.

Counter-intuitively, this is the way the LA Leggers' lead coach taught novices to train for the marathon. Start running for one minute and walking for one minute. Continue to build it up, two minutes' running and one minute's walking, three minutes' running and one minute's walking and on until you get to nine running and one walking. Then, on the day, set your pace at nine minutes' running, one walking.

At first, Heather found it incredibly difficult to walk for a minute after just nine minutes, when everyone else was setting a faster pace and running past her. However, by mile 18, when every other first-time runner was 'hitting the wall' and slowing down, she was just hitting her stride and starting to overtake everyone who'd passed her in the first part of the race. Heather finished with a very credible time of just over four hours 48 minutes.

RIDING THE WAVES

Simon: The metaphor of running our race well is well known, but at the start of this book we introduced a different way of thinking about leading the millennial way: windsurfers navigating the incredible waves made and faced by our millennial generation en masse. Throughout, we have seen the incredible strength that millennial leaders already have to face the challenges that are ahead, but have also introduced you to some new tools and approaches that will enable you to ride higher and higher waves.

The reality of leadership for the millennial generation is this. The waves are not going to get any smaller or less difficult to ride, but you can learn not to be daunted by them and, instead, to harness them, gain momentum and surf with style.

AT THE END OF THE DAY

Simon: Running, windsurfing, leading: it all takes endurance and, as we have seen, we are going to make mistakes, fall down and need to get back up again.

While writing this book, the phrase 'at the end of the day' has been buzzing around my head. For some of you, it may conjure images of the wonderful West End show, *Les Misérables*. In the show, the peasants sing the familiar lines that tell of the entrapment, hopelessness and pain of living in poverty; that at the end of each day you are just a day older, a day poorer. At the end of the day, you just have one day less to be living.

Some days as a leader feel like that. But some days, the 'end of the day' feels different.

I was recently at a board meeting where one member kept using this phrase. 'At the end of the day,' he began, 'there are people still living in poverty . . . At the end of the day, there is so much more to be accomplished, so much that can be transformed . . . At the end of the day, there is only one thing that matters. Will you finish well?'

It made me think. At the end of the day, does every day count?

Throughout your leadership journey, as your head hits the pillow each night and another day comes to an end, has it been 'one day less to be living' or a day living life in all its fullness, leading those around you into a fuller experience of life? Have you been a leader who is fully who you are, giving all that you have to give?

We know which one we want it to be for us, and that makes the effort of *leading – the millennial way* an adventure worth pursuing.

More about our research

The primary interest in undertaking this research was to inform the character-based leadership development of Christians who are working in all sectors of society. This original definition of focus stemmed simply from the fact that many of the Forge Leadership founder Simon Barrington's contemporaries in leadership were from the Christian sector. However, as the research progressed, we began to identify patterns that had implications for a generation, without being limited to individuals with a faith.

We were challenged by the lack of emerging leaders taking up significant roles across society, while at the same time showing evidence of inherent security in their own identities, deep integrity, the strength of character to last the course, as well as the insight required to take hard decisions and therefore be able to influence the transformation of the whole of society.

The vast majority of the research was focused on millennials' leadership development, the culture they were creating, the opportunities and challenges they faced, and their identities as leaders. A small number of questions focused on their Christian faith.

As we have dialogued the results of this research with leaders of all faiths and none in a diverse cross section of public and private sector organizations, we have encountered a remarkable resonance and empathy with our findings from these leaders. We are confident, therefore, that they will resonate with you too and that we can all learn from them as indicators of how millennials are leading and how they intend to lead going forward.

You can download a full copy of the research report at <www.millennial-leader.com/research>

Notes

1 THE GROUND IS SHIFTING

1 Laloux, F., 2014. *Reinventing Organizations: A Guide to Creating Organizations Inspired by the Next Stage of Human Consciousness.* Brussels: Nelson Parker, p. 44.

2 Deloitte, 2016. 'The 2016 Deloitte Millennial Survey' [online]. Available at: <www2.deloitte.com/content/dam/Deloitte/global/Documents/About-Deloitte/gx-millenial-survey-2016-exec-summary.pdf> [accessed January 2019].

3 Sachs, A., and Kundu, A., 2015. 'The Unfinished Business of Organizational Transition' [online]. Available at: <www.thoughtworks.com/insights/blog/unfinished-business-organizational-transformation> [accessed July 2018].

2 MARKS OF THE MILLENNIAL ORGANIZATION - KNOWING YOUR LEADERSHIP LANDSCAPE

1 Catmull, E., 2008. 'How Pixar Fosters Collective Creativity' [online]. Available at: <https://hbr.org/2008/09/how-pixar-fosters-collective-creativity> [accessed July 2018].

2 Cranfield School of Management and The Doughty Centre for Corporate Responsibility, 2014. 'Combining Profit and Purpose' [online]. Available at: <www.cokecce.com/system/file_resources/210/W21883_TL_Report_A4_FINAL.pdf> [accessed January 2019].

3 Forge Leadership Podcast [online]. Available at: <https://forge-leadership.com/forge-leadership-podcast/> [accessed 2018].

4 Kaifi, B., Nafei, W., and Kaifi, M., 2012. 'A Multi-Generational Workforce: Managing and Understanding Millennials', *International Journal of Business and Management*, 7 (24), p. 89.

5 Srivastava, M., and Banerjee, P., 2016. 'Understanding Gen Y: The Motivations, Values and Beliefs', *Journal of Management Research*, 16 (3), p. 151.

6 Chou, S., 2012. 'Millennials in the Workplace: A Conceptual Analysis of Millennials' Leadership and Followership Styles', *International Journal of Human Resource Studies*, 2 (2), p. 75.

7 Murray, A., (2011). 'Mind the Gap: Technology, Millennial Leadership and the Cross-Generational Workforce', *The Australian Library Journal*, 60 (1), p. 54.

8 Virtuali, 2015. 'Engaging Millennials through Leadership Development' [online]. Available at: <https://docplayer.net/65296968-Engaging-millennials-through-leadership-development.html> [accessed January 2019].

9 Gates, B., 1999. *Business @ the Speed of Thought: Using a Digital Nervous System*. New York: Warner Books.

10 Brafman, O., and Beckstrom, R., 2006. *The Starfish and the Spider: The Unstoppable Power of Leaderless Organizations*. New York: Portfolio (Penguin Group, USA).

11 'Knowledge, Trust, Credibility and a Focus on Results – Are They Factors that Disrupt or Help Society Evolve?' [online]. Available at: <http://wirearchy.com/2014/02/24/knowledge-trust-credibility-and-a-focus-on-results-are-they-factors-that-disrupt-or-help-society-evolve/> [accessed November 2018].

12 'What Is Wirearchy?' [online] Available at <http://wirearchy.com/what-is-wirearchy/> [accessed November 2018].

13 Christensen, C., 1997. *The Innovator's Dilemma: When New Technologies Cause Great Firms to Fail*. Boston, Mass.: Harvard Business Review Press.

14 Davenport, T., 2009. 'How to Design Smart Business Experiments' [online]. Available at: <https://hbr.org/2009/02/how-to-design-smart-business-experiments> [accessed July 2018].

15 Weakley, K., 2016. 'FRSB Report into Olive Cooke Highly Critical of Data Sharing by Charities' [online]. Available at: <www.civilsociety.co.uk/news/frsb-report-into-olive-cooke-highly-critical-of-data-sharing-by-charities.html> [accessed November 2018].

16 EU GDPR [online]. Available at: <https://eugdpr.org> [accessed November 2018].

17 Patagonia [online]. Available at: <https://eu.patagonia.com/gb/en/home/> [accessed November 2018].

18 Rhoads, R., 2015. 'Restoring Burnout Millennial Ministry Leaders within a Western North American Digital Society' [online]. Available at: <https://digitalcommons.georgefox.edu/dmin/98/> Doctor of Ministry, George Fox University.

19 Gallup, 2016. 'How Millennials Want to Work and Live' [online]. Available at: <www.gallup.com/workplace/238073/millennials-work-live.aspx> [accessed January 2019].

20 Moritz, B., 2014. 'The U.S. Chairman of PWC on Keeping Millennials Engaged' [online]. Available at: <https://hbr.org/2014/11/the-us-chairman-of-pwc-on-keeping-millennials-engaged> [accessed July 2018].

21 Sinek, S., 2014. 'Why Good Leaders Make You Feel Safe' [online]. Available at: <www.ted.com/talks/simon_sinek_why_good_leaders_make_you_feel_safe/transcript#t-663977> [accessed July 2018].

3 HOW AND WHY YOU HAVE BEEN MISUNDERSTOOD

1 Srivastava, M. and Banerjee, P., 2016. 'Understanding Gen Y: The Motivations, Values and Beliefs', *Journal of Management Research*, 16 (3), p. 148.

2 University of Notre Dame, 2017. 'Attract Emerging Leaders with Purpose, not Perks' [online]. Available at: <https://ethicalleadership.nd.edu/news/attract-emerging-leaders-with-purpose-not-perks/> [accessed January 2019].

3 Hobart, B. and Sendek, H., 2014. *Gen Y Now: Millennials and the Evolution of Leadership.* San Francisco, Calif.: John Wiley & Sons, p. 33.

4 Hobart and Sendek. *Gen Y Now*, pp. 37–75.

5 Hobart and Sendek. *Gen Y Now*, p. 25.

6 *The Economist*, 2014. 'Proof that You Should Get a Life' [online]. Available at: <www.economist.com/free-exchange/2014/12/09/proof-that-you-should-get-a-life> [accessed July 2018].

7 Montes, J., 2017. *Millennial Workforce: Cracking the Code to Generation Y in Your Company.* Kindle edition, Lulu Publishing Services.

5 IDENTITY - IT'S NOT WHO YOU KNOW, IT'S WHO YOU *ARE*

1 Institute of Directors, 2018. 'Karen Blackett on Authentic Leadership and Creating Opportunity' [online]. Available at: <www.director.co.uk/karen-blackett-on-authentic-leadership-and-creating-opportunity/> [accessed July 2018].

2 Luft, J. and Ingham, H., 1955. 'The Johari Window, a Graphic Model of Interpersonal Awareness'. Proceedings of the western training laboratory in group development. Los Angeles, Calif.: University of California.

3 Brown, B., 2017. 'High Lonesome: A Spiritual Crisis', *Braving the Wilderness: The Quest for True Belonging and the Courage to Stand Alone.* Kindle edition, Ebury Digital, location 696, section 3.

4 Maxwell, J., 2014. 'Insecurity: An Explosive Quality in the Life of a Leader' [online]. <http://blog.johnmaxwell.com/blog/insecurity-an-explosive-quality-in-the-life-of-a-leader> [accessed October 2018].

5 Brown, B., 2012. *Daring Greatly: How the Courage to Be Vulnerable Transforms the Way We Live, Love, Parent, and Lead.* London: Penguin, p. 34.

6 Forge Leadership Podcast [online]. Available at: <https://forge-leadership.com/2018/01/19/forge-leadership-podcast-episode-11-bev-kauffeldt/> [accessed 2018].

6 INTEGRITY – WHY GOODNESS CAN BE MORE VALUABLE THAN GREATNESS

1 Hobart, B. and Sendek, H., 2014. *Gen Y Now: Millennials and the Evolution of Leadership.* San Francisco, Calif.: John Wiley & Sons, p. 6.

2 Kouzes, J. and Posner, B., 2007. *The Leadership Challenge*, 4th edn. San Francisco, Calif.: John Wiley & Sons, p. 49.

3 Kouzes and Posner. *The Leadership Challenge*, p. 50.

4 Kahler, T., 1979. *Process Therapy in Brief: The clinical application of miniscript.* Little Rock, Ark.: Human Development Publications.

5 Clinton, R., 2012. *The Making of a Leader: Recognizing the Lessons and Stages of Leadership Development.* Colorado Springs, Colo.: NavPress, p. 138.

6 Clear, J., 2016. 'My 2016 Integrity Report' [online]. Available at: <https://jamesclear.com/2016-integrity-report> [accessed July 2018].

7 Murray, A., 2011. 'Mind the Gap: Technology, Millennial leadership and the Cross-Generational Workforce', *The Australian Library Journal*, 60 (1), pp. 54–65.

8 Farrell, L., and Hurt, A., 2014. 'Training the Millennial Generation: Implications for Organizational Climate', *Journal of Organizational Learning and Leadership,* 12 (1), pp. 47–60.

7 INNER STRENGTH

1 Quoted by Mike Pilavachi <https://twitter.com/mikepilav> 31 March 2018 [accessed November 2018].

2 Fries, K., 2017. '4 Ways to Help Millennial Leaders Overcome Mental Health Problems' [online]. Available at: <www.forbes.com/sites/kimberlyfries/2017/12/18/4-ways-to-help-millennial-leaders-overcome-mental-health-problems/> [accessed January 2018].

3 Duncan, D., 2017. *The Art of Daily Resilience: How to Develop a Durable Spirit.* Oxford: Monarch (Lion Hudson), p. 20.

4 *Financial Times*, 2013. 'Work, Rest and Pray' [online]. Available at: <www.ft.com/content/9360a59e-5abb-11e2-bc93-00144feab49a> [accessed September 2018].

8 INSIGHT

1 Forge Leadership Podcast [online]. Available at: <https://forge-leader ship.com/2018/03/23/episode-20-baroness-caroline-cox/> [accessed January 2019].

9 TRANSFORMING INFLUENCE

1 Best Companies, 2018. 'The Message Trust' [online]. Available at: <www.b.co.uk/company-profile/?the-message-trust-99576> [accessed April 2018].

10 TRANSFORMING CULTURE

1 Schein, E., 2016. *Organizational Culture and Leadership*, 5th edn. San Francisco, Calif.: Jossey-Bass (John Wiley & Sons), p. 267.

2 Godin, S., 2011. *Tribes: We Need You to Lead Us.* London: Piatkus (Little, Brown), p. 116.

3 Karin Ahlbäck, K., Fahrbach, C., and Muraka, M., 2017. 'How to Create an Agile Organization' [online]. Available at: <www.mckinsey. com/business-functions/organization/our-insights/how-to-create-an-agile-organization> [accessed July 2018].

4 Hines, A., 2011. 'A Dozen Surprises about the Future of Work', *Employment Relations Today*, 38 (1).

5 Murphy, W., 2012. 'Reverse Mentoring at Work: Fostering Cross-Generational Learning and Developing Millennial Leaders', *Human Resource Management*, 51 (4).

6 Barna Group, 2014. *Making Space for Millennials: A Blueprint for Your Culture, Ministry, Leadership and Facilities.* Ventura, Calif.: Barna Group.

7 Forge Leadership Podcast [online]. Available at: <https://forge-leader ship.com/2018/02/16/forge-leadership-podcast-episode-15-rev-hugh-osgood/> [accessed January 2019].

8 Magree, J., 2017. 'Minding Minds at Work' [online]. Available at: <http://blog.deloitte.com.au/minding-minds-work-mental-health-stigma/> [accessed July 2018].

9 Meyer, E., 2016. *The Culture Map: Decoding How People Think, Lead, and Get Things Done Across Cultures.* New York: Public Affairs (Perseus Books Group), p. 252.

10 Laloux, F., 2014. *Reinventing Organizations: A Guide to Creating Organizations Inspired by the Next Stage of Human Consciousness.* Brussels: Nelson Parker, p. 134.

11 A FINAL CHALLENGE – TO FINISH WELL

1 Soffel, J., 2015. 'Which Leaders Do Millennials Admire the Most?' [online]. Available at: <www.weforum.org/agenda/2015/10/which-leaders-do-millennials-admire-the-most/> [accessed July 2018].

2 CNN Business, 2010. '100 Years Old – and Still Working!' [online]. Available at: <www.youtube.com/watch?v=yKTRY3Xm940> [accessed July 2018].

3 Clinton, J. R., 1995. *Focused Lives: Inspirational Life Changing Lessons from Eight Effective Christian Leaders Who Finished Well.* Zeeland, Mich.: Barnabas Publishing.